Process Philosophy

Process Philosophy

A Synthesis

Bart Nooteboom

ANTHEM PRESS

Anthem Press
An imprint of Wimbledon Publishing Company
www.anthempress.com

This edition first published in UK and USA 2025
by ANTHEM PRESS
75–76 Blackfriars Road, London SE1 8HA, UK
or PO Box 9779, London SW19 7ZG, UK
and
244 Madison Ave #116, New York, NY 10016, USA

First published in the UK and USA by Anthem Press in 2021

Copyright © Bart Nooteboom 2025

The author asserts the moral right to be identified as the author of this work.

All rights reserved. Without limiting the rights under copyright reserved above,
no part of this publication may be reproduced, stored or introduced into
a retrieval system, or transmitted, in any form or by any means
(electronic, mechanical, photocopying, recording or otherwise),
without the prior written permission of both the copyright
owner and the above publisher of this book.

British Library Cataloguing-in-Publication Data
A catalogue record for this book is available from the British Library.

Library of Congress Control Number: 2024943691

ISBN-13: 978-1-83999-373-2 (Pbk)
ISBN-10: 1-83999-373-1 (Pbk)

Cover credit: Shutterstock\images

This title is also available as an e-book.

CONTENTS

Preface vii
Foreword by Patricia de Sá Freire ix

Introduction: Definition of Terms, Purpose and Summary 1

1. Evolution 15
2. Learning and Truth 29
3. Language 53
4. Individual and Society 67
5. Morality and Ethics 87

Conclusions 113
References 115
Index 123

PREFACE

In my career as a scholar of innovation and organisation, I was professionally interested in processes of change, and was struck by the ubiquity of change in different fields of science and philosophy, and became intrigued by the question what they might have in common. I have been reading philosophy since I was 13, and was interested in particular in philosophies of change, finding that the theme was more in evidence in Eastern than in Western philosophy. After many years of study, I came to this book, discussing forms of change and seeking connections.

FOREWORD

I thank Dr Bart Nooteboom for the honourable invitation to write these few pages as a foreword to his book. In this newest book, based on an interdisciplinary vision brought about by the dialogue between philosophy and organisational studies, the author delves into human sociocultural relations, among other matters, helping to recover the focus on the individual with microfoundations in a technological era, and offers foundations for consistent research and projects on the organisational level.

Upon reading Professor Bart Nooteboom's book, my reaction was the pleasant satisfaction of identifying that the themes indispensable to the establishment of organisational resilience and the configuration of contemporary governance models (multilevel governance and governance of learning and knowledge) will have, starting from the launch of this book, a fundamental support. Various elements covered in this book are multilevel governance mechanisms, such as intra- and inter-organisational learning networks, organisational and individual, management of change processes and the creation of human knowledge, and the elements of trust and collaboration for the entire system to cohere.

In the world of disruptive digital transformations, the focus has been on technological changes and integrations, but the adaptive advantages inherent to successful organisations are the result of collaboration between autonomous individuals capable of learning and adapting to multilevel learning networks.

It is clear that despite the individuality of the subjects, they are all integrated into the general program of *Homo sapiens* and also into more limited programming frameworks, such as the cultures to which they belong. But this limitation is illusory, since the subjects are connected to the organisational network, translating information and reinterpreting it, returning it to the environment from their personal connections, and strengthening the cultural network from their view and interpretation of the world. In other words, this phenomenon of interactive construction between the environment and the individual is linked to other phenomena, within a network of space-time connections.

When one tries to understand the process that leads individuals to make the decision to collaborate or not with peers, it is realised that one can no longer look at those individuals as autonomous. A system emerges with complex structures, and with interwoven elements, and that, after we perceive the extent of its complexity, makes us capable of dealing with the real and of dialoguing and negotiating with it.

Looking with a systemic view at the complexity inherent to an individual's cognitive process is to perceive the infinite play of inter-feedback between cognition and environment. To really understand and put in order the complex phenomena intrinsic to the social process, it is necessary to perceive the challenges of human experiences from the perspective of the individual, selecting the elements of order and certainty, which will help to clarify, distinguish and hierarchise the formal phenomena. One must recognise the restlessness, the disorder, the ambiguity, the paradoxical, and the uncertain that make up the elements that are part of this complex open system called the human being, and its process of knowing the world in order to decide about it.

It is understood that human knowledge is built from the relationships experienced within the complex system of relationships between them, the environment and the other participants in the network of connections: their perceptions, interpretations, emotions and reactions. And, to understand the individual, the high-performance teams and the organisational machine in its complexity, they should no longer be perceived as a simple summation of their behavioural expressions, but rather as a being in self-organisation, woven by events, actions, emotions, interactions, determinations and chance.

This book warns that what individuals know affects and is affected by what they are able to perceive in the environment. The way they conceptualise and classify what they perceive ends up influencing their way of reasoning about the relationships they experience, leading them to make decisions consistent not with the result intended by a dominant paradigm, but with what they have discovered.

After reading this book, leaders will be made aware that decision-making is an individual cognitive process, but that it also depends on the environment around the subjects because individuals are possessed by the environment in some way, since it is the environment that dictates the rules for their self-organisation, limiting or providing opportunities for their cognitive development. And, reciprocally, the individuals affect the characteristics of the environment in which they are inserted, actively participating in its construction and reinforcing its beliefs, because, if they do not accept them as rules, they will enter into a state of defence, moving themselves away or provoking their own withdrawal. An understanding will be reached that the decision to collaborate or not with the development of the collective good is first made internally to the individuals and only then they come together in a collaborative group in order to carry out as a common movement the transfer of knowledge into the organisation's practice.

Besides other important points, the book leads us to foresee that the way to make a conscious (that takes into account all the determining variables) and committed (to the intended results) decision goes through the individual cognitive system but, for it to be applied in the organisational practice, one will need to collaborate and negotiate with other individuals and with cultural characteristics that may enhance or block the achievement process. So, to make a decision, individuals must become aware of their own complex relationship with the environment and other people.

In this way, becoming aware of reality is seen as one of the important stages of cognitive development, to enable the perception of disagreements, relationships of trust and the motivations that lie behind relationships. From the point of view of philosophy, the individuals' action in the world is a dynamic of construction of their own being, it is their presence and their possibilities of coming to be something else in the next moment, and it is dependent on their relations with the phenomena perceived in the environment. It is a dynamics of continuous structuring, in which states, passages and places are exchanged.

This subject, which is existence, is a project of being able to be something else in the future, that is, it is a project of what is to come. All the concretisations in the existence of a being exert an action expressed together, never occurring as being or a way of being isolated, because every being is always being-with; even in solitude and isolation, presence is always co-presence, the world is always shared, living is always coexistence.

But how can this process be understood? In their actions when coming into contact with a new phenomenon in the environment (and the author brings us several cases in his works as examples), the individuals seek, in their memory, recorded representations that help them to give meaning – to interpret – to their current experience. When identifying something 'similar' in their memory, they classify the new phenomenon based on similarities. Then, a new relationship is established, and if the phenomenon behaves as expected, that is, like the one already registered in their memory, nothing will change, and the mental model will be confirmed, rooting their beliefs and values more deeply. However, if the new events do not proceed as expected, the individuals are forced to leave their comfort zone and change their mental models by adopting new elements from their environment.

But these new elements are not so easily incorporated; on the contrary, the individuals react to changes they do not recognise, which can generate a state of organisational crisis through the paralysis of the productive flow, focusing on the defence of their comfort zone – which means to accomplish what is already known and accepted by the group. The group instinctively concentrates its energies on its self-defence, in the search for the previously existing balance, starting a long path of instability, until the end of the dynamics of adaptation to the adopted changes.

Dr Bart Nooteboom presents us with a beautiful book about the essential elements to be considered for the governance and management of these human and sociocultural relations so as to innovate but not reach the state of crisis.

I congratulate Dr Bart Nooteboom and wish everyone a good reading.

Patricia de Sá Freire
Knowledge Integration and Governance Engineering Center,
ENGIN/UFSC/CNPQ

INTRODUCTION: DEFINITION OF TERMS, PURPOSE AND SUMMARY

Philosophical Orientation

Practical philosophy asks what to do with life, while taking responsibility for one's role in society (Hubert Dethier 1993, 525). From philosophical pragmatism (Peirce, James and Dewey, see Malachowski 2013) I adopt the view that ideas are to be evaluated by the implications they have for practical life. Peirce, an early pragmatist, 'called Jesus a pragmatist and proposed that the saying "By their fruits ye shall know them" was an early version of the pragmatic maxim' (Nicholson 2013, 251).

Philosophers call this orientation towards a goal *intentionality*. Even microbes have it, in moving towards a source of food. People, in contrast with most animals, have 'second-order intentions' (Okrent 2013, 150), in seeing their intentions as their own, in self-awareness and possibly changing them. This allows people to consider not only what is actual but also what is possible, and to consider one's death. In a practice, things are connected, and this leads to a view of the world as a connected whole. Practices change, in adaptation to a changing world, and this leads to a process view. We come to the world with a potential for development of ideas in interaction with things in the world, especially people.

With pragmatism, focusing on the usefulness of individual things, one may neglect the wider system, in not seeing the wood for the trees. Something that is useful for a single thing may be harmful to the system it is in. Damage to the natural environment is an obvious example. This is akin to the notion, in economics, of 'externality': The environment is taken for granted, and one is unable to take into account the cost of pollution. One neglects the totality of the environment.

A wider task of philosophy is to discuss issues that are otherwise not questioned, are taken for granted, in daily life and science, of which there are many that we are hardly aware of. An example is in the understanding of puzzles that arise in modern physics, discussed below.

The puzzles yield the urge to come up with new ideas, in new thought, as pursued, for example, by Nietzsche, Heidegger, Foucault, Derrida and Deleuze. In other words: Philosophy tinkers with fundamentals. The problem with this, this looking for what underlies fundamentals, is that it is not clear what the fundamentals of it are. When asked what philosophy is, my granddaughter said that it is about questions to which there are no answers. It is riding a horse which is not there. It is a precarious affair that demands modesty. With a paucity of empirical grounding, philosophy is a matter of debate, with arguments from experience and science to make it plausible. In my view, which I share with Hubert Dethier (1993, 529), life, and the philosophy of it, is an endless attempt to transcend what is given, in knowledge and rules. It is *imperfection on the move*. Such change constitutes human purpose itself, gives meaning to life, is the human condition. That requires spirit, courage, resilience and, paradoxically, both perseverance and flexibility. However, while Deleuze, for example, wants to escape from common sense, I want to connect to it while going beyond it.

A challenge for philosophy is to contribute to an understanding of modern physics: relativity theories, quantum mechanics and attempts to bring the two together, in theories of 'Quantum Gravity' (Rovelli 2016). The levels of nature studied in modern physics, of elementary particles and fields, and in this book the level of people in society, are widely different. What is the connection? Is there similarity? Does there need to be? The question is not only whether philosophy can contribute to an understanding of modern physics, but also whether it can itself employ the logic, the way of thinking, the mathematics that emerges from that physics, concerning the relation between particles and fields, in physics, and here between people and social fields. In a later chapter on language I ask whether the realisation of one of many possible meanings of a word that arises when it is connected with other words in a sentence can be compared to the 'collapse' of a cloud of probabilities of the position of an elementary particle to a specific position upon the collision with another particle, in the complementarity view of the 'Copenhagen Interpretation' in physics.

I do find it interesting that, like the present book, modern physics yields a process theory, with universal and ongoing movement, in quantum theory, and a relational view, where elementary particles, such as electrons, exist only in interaction with others. The interaction consists of the exchange of another particle. Two electrons repulse each other in the exchange of a photon. In this book, people are constituted in interaction with each other: in isolation, people cannot flourish. People exchange meanings, in communication. How useful is this comparison? Is it a metaphor? Can it serve as a model? How far does the comparison go? There are fundamental differences. All particles of a certain kind are identical. People are not. Some kinds of particles cannot interact with all other kinds. People can, more or less.

Fritjof Capra (1975) claimed that the apparent mysteries in modern physics are similar to those of ancient Eastern mysticism, in particular Taoism, which held that opposites cohere, are one, such as in the physical notion of complementarity where elementary particles are both particles and waves of probabilities of their locations. Things can literally be neither here nor there. Like modern physics, Buddhism and Taoism are process views: everything flows. Also, they both claim that everything is connected to everything else. The Eastern mystics claim direct apprehension of 'the One' that encompasses all, in absolute knowledge, without concepts and language, let alone theory. Science, by contrast, is always based on basic assumptions, as a point of departure for the deduction, in a theory, of possible phenomena, which are subjected to experiment, and form the basis for critical debate among colleagues. In Chapter 3 of this book, in which I discuss knowledge and learning, I say that looking in any direction one cannot at the same time look in all other directions. Scientific knowledge is therefore never absolute and always partial, never 'the one', and subject to development.

Capra said (Capra 1975, 47), concerning mysticism, 'the environment is experienced in a direct way without the filter of conceptual thinking'. It sounds like thinking without thinking. How can I say, in language, that language is illusory? Should I only write *haiku's?* I can see limitations and distortions in knowledge and language, and indeed I will discuss them in this book, but I cannot just drop argument and dissolve myself in silent contemplation. To compare ideas from modern physics with those of Eastern mysticism, does that involve explanation or mere putting on new labels to our ignorance? I have read the Taoist 'I Ching', the book of changes (Wilhelm 2003), and it is intriguing but also seems capricious, without critical argument or discussion of different views and interpretations. Does Eastern mysticism help to understand physics, or is it the other way around: Does physics help to legitimise Eastern mysticism? To me, in order to help our understanding of physics, the mysticism needs to be put into words to produce argument and criticism, and then it no longer is mysticism.

There is a tendency, in 'postmodern' philosophy, to turn away from familiar ideas of truth, subject, identity, causality, meaning, reference and representation. But those concepts came up because we needed them, and we use them all the time, in practical daily life. There are indeed philosophical problems with them, but we can salvage some of them with some twists. For example, in Chapter 3, I will maintain the notion of reference, in an intentional, not ontological, sense, where people intend to refer, aside from the question whether they actually do so, and utilise the notion of 'sense' as an additional dimension of meaning: achieving the intended reference. In my theory of knowledge and language I maintain the notion of 'representation', not as an a priori benchmark we compare and judge observations with, but as an a posteriori, tacit, largely subconscious construction of neuronal networks in the brain that are constructed in action, and guide our subsequent conduct, largely subconsciously.

Truth as correspondence with objective reality is problematic, but we need it, or something like it, in wanting to know whether what Corona experts say is 'true', for example. Life depends on it. As I will discuss later, we can still use the notion of truth in the form of 'warranted assertibility', proposed by John Dewey. Objective truth cannot be achieved, but one can still come up with 'warrants' in the form of facts to the extent we can agree upon them, logic, plausibility, defined as coherence with other parts of accepted knowledge, and the degree to which something 'works' in its application. The latter is where pragmatism comes in.

I want to maintain, because we cannot do without, the notion of 'subject' as the one, me, you, who perceives, feels and acts. It is not necessarily the idea of a self that is formed outside the world, somehow, and looks at it from outside, as a spectator. One can see it as arising and developing in action in the world and thus not being independent from it. In particular, as argued by G. H. Mead (2011), the self arises in interaction with others, in sending off bodily gestures, sounds and linguistic expressions that trigger response in the other, one's observation of that response, and one's response to that. One can see 'identity' not as a fixed essence, who one 'really' is, but as work in progress, in a process of adaptation, with change within the bounds of inherited potential.

I don't see how we can do without the notion of 'causality'. But causality can mean different things. It is not necessarily mechanical push or transmission. It can be more than purely formal succession of cause and effect. One view of causation was that of a law of nature that under certain conditions generates outcomes. More complicated, it has been seen as a mechanism, with an interaction between components that produces outcomes. That may sound mechanical, but I am not sure what that means. Are fields of force mechanical? Magnetism and electrical repulsion/attraction? A cause produces an outcome, perhaps indirectly via an intermediate cause, and in concert with other causes. This can be multilevel, where a mechanism on the lower level can be a component on a higher level. A body is made up of organs, made up of cells, made up of molecules, made up of .... There may be other parts that belong to the whole, while they are not part of the mechanism of the part in question, such as doors on a car that are not part of the car's engine (Craver, 2007). Fundamentalists claim that 'real' causality is found only when 'educed' to the most fundamental level. However, non-fundamental explanations are needed for most phenomena. We cannot make a theory of the brain that is at odds with how neurons work, on the fundamental level, but we are far from explaining thought on the basis only of how neurons work. Later, I will discuss Aristotle's multiple causality of action.

Explanation can be vertical, by going into underlying processes, which is the 'fundamental' way, or horizontal, in adding complementary perspectives. For example, suppose we want to explain the functioning of a scientific group. Vertically, one can investigate cognitive processes that underlie mutual (mis)understanding. Horizontally, one can add a perspective of the effects of network structure of relations between the scientists. Features of network structure are discussed later in this book. A third perspective is that of behavioural traits such as rivalry in the race for reputation or funding. Such horizontal connection is not necessarily less valid than the vertical deepening.

There can be 'negative', inhibitory causation in preventing something to occur. When the inhibition is lifted, the phenomenon occurs. There are things that can hasten or slow down a process, but are not needed for it, such as a catalyst in a chemical process. The old notion of a final cause, something a thing strives for or moves towards, may not be valid in inanimate nature, but it is still a cause of human and animal action. In pragmatism, the outcome that a cause is expected to produce is salient. That depends on the purpose of an action, the final cause.

The problem with purely conceptual analysis in philosophy is the paucity of empirical grounding, evidence. Such evidence may be found to some extent in anthropological studies (Liisberg 2015), or in other scientific disciplines such as sociology, psychology, political science and economics.

I do grant that much needs to be done also on conceptual matters to help understand the evidence and, for example, see what applies generally and what locally, and why. This connects with the perennial issue of universals or general concepts applying across all individuals and contexts, the particular cases in which they manifest themselves. To understand the human being and society we need general concepts, but as Aristotle already claimed, in contrast with Plato, the general, or universal, exists only in its particulars and exists by itself, as an essence, only conceptually. An essence, in the form of a Platonic idea, is universal and eternal. By an 'essence' I understand a feature that something must have for it to belong to a category. It entails the absence of any process of change, and I find that difficult to imagine. I think that mostly it is a chimera. General ideas change as new instances or anomalies arise.

For an animal, I suppose its 'essence' would be its DNA. For a use object, such as a chair, it would be its use. But many things could be used for a chair. We can have a prototype (Rosch 1978) of a chair, a typical chair, but not an essence. A category has been said to have a *radial* structure, with a core of typical or prototypical cases, surrounded by non-prototypical and sometimes dubious cases. Do birds have an essence? A robin is a prototype for the English, I am told, and a sparrow for the Dutch. Some birds sing, such as a blackbird, some swim, such as a duck, some prey on animals, such as a buzzard, some don't fly, such as an ostrich, some migrate, such as geese, some fly in a flock, such as starlings. On the other hand, all birds do have two legs, two eyes and a beak and lay eggs. But other animals also have two legs and eyes. A platypus has a beak and lays eggs. Tsoukas and Chia (2002) use the example of lying: there are peripheral, debatable cases of white lies, social lies, mistakes, errors and jokes.

Categories shift, because everything, physical and conceptual, interacts with its environment and adapts to it, within boundaries of its potential, not everything can be foreseen, and variations and boundary cases are explored of existing categories to accommodate change, until the need and insight arise for new, separate categories.

A problem with a general concept or universal is that it tempts us to ignore the differences between the individuals belonging to it, and the need to differentiate accordingly. This is noted, for example, by Deleuze and Bergson. We do need generalisation, as practically necessary for actions with particular objects, to generalise experience and benefit from transferring it. This occurs in countless activities – such as elevator maintenance, picking up a stone to throw, a lost child to find, an arrow to intercept, a type of prey to be hunted – and such actions are needed for survival, and make us develop generalised ideas in that action. There, we see things 'as' something. We can see a cat as a mouse-catching animal. Depending on the context we can see things in many different ways. We should somehow be able to practice a general concept and remain aware of the differences within and between its manifestations.

The idea that a universal can exist only as a conceptual construct came to be known as *nominalism*, as opposed to the Platonic *realistic* claim that it 'really' exists, in some realm that transcends the world as we experience it, in all its complexity and variability, and are absolute, that is, constant and valid everywhere, regardless of context such as culture or climate. As a matter of principle, to avoid parochial bias and imperialist thought, I assume that to a greater or lesser extent all individual manifestations are context-dependent, and the challenge is to find out to what extent they are general. In other words, I seek the general but avoid claims of universality, and hence I am a nominalist.

From *object-oriented ontology* (Garcia 2014; Harman 2018), I take that an object has an interior ('what is in it') and an exterior ('what it is in') in interaction with other objects, in its outward manifestation and influence from outside. Its identity arises from a certain durable coherence within it. That coherence lies in causation between elements of it and effects from outside. A thing has a certain potential or capacity to operate and develop. DNA is an example. The coherent whole has properties that the parts do not have. To maintain its order, the object must preserve a balance between its parts and its corresponding interaction with the environment. Manuel DeLanda (2016, 180) made a distinction between the tendency and the capacity of an object. A tendency is repetitive, limited in its variation, while capacities are more like skills, flexible and adaptive, but also limited, in their potential to affect and be affected. As a result of this capacity, things are not static but changing, and I want to understand that, in process philosophy.

Hegel showed that we get to know something in its failures or limits. That is also how thought and capability work: they are learned by the person or theory bumping into the consequences of its shortcomings. That is also the basis of science. Gaston Bachelard (1950) said that nature can shout 'no' to our ideas. I learned from Johnston (2008) that the arch-idealist Fichte recognized that in action a shock (an 'Anstoss', in German) can literally yield a 'push', affecting and shifting ideas. To use a term from Derrida, experience 'deconstructs' knowledge. That does not mean, however, that all our errors are caught out.

This Book

The aim of the present book is to give a synthesis of ideas about change, bringing together views from different philosophers and myself, spread out in earlier work. I aim to see how one can take a process view of various features of humanity, such as knowledge, language, relations between people, and morality, and how, vice versa, that might contribute to process philosophy in general. The coherence between the book's parts is not just a matter of logical consistency, but also of mutual support, as a house of cards: Arguments rest upon each other. I aim for clarification, untangling complexity and avoiding unnecessary vagueness. I don't want to hang on to a decrepit Enlightenment or Cartesian illusion of complete clarity: Our language is too imperfect for that, and often our thinking is myopic, ambiguous and biased. But discourse, and hence mutual understanding, is crucial and to enable that we should be as clear as possible. It is often difficult to present philosophical issues in ordinary language, and the temptation arises to invent new words, but this often yields obscurity, as I find in reading Heidegger and Deleuze, so one should take only gingerly steps away from ordinary language, not to be unnecessarily unclear.

A book is never finished. One can think of it as a tree that spreads out into ever new branches. Alternatively, one can think of it as a *rhizome*, proposed by Deleuze and Guattari (1991), which is a root or root system with nodes from which new shoots can rise up, as with mushrooms. As one progresses along the book, seen as such a root, upon return to a node on it, one can find new ideas springing up, and this can go on. The book mushrooms.

The purpose of this book is to indicate how in all their differences, views from different fields connect, in seeing things as change, in particular the individual as a social animal that is constituted in interaction with things and people in the world, but does that along a unique path of life, by which it develops into an individual. The central theme, of individual and society, in Chapter 4, goes back to Aristotle, who saw the human being as a 'political', that is, social, animal. I take a process view, of evolution, knowledge, morality, ethics and language. A motivation for this book lies in the view that there are unexplored connections between what has been said about these forms of change, and I think that there is both a desire and an opportunity, for both mature philosophers and students, and a wider public, for a synthesis. I take a dynamic view of the human being, in its evolution as a species (phylogenesis) as well as its development during its life (ontogenesis), and of knowledge, in learning and innovation, of language, in meaning change, of relations between people, and of morality.

Since the issues discussed in this book depend on each other, it is not directly clear where to begin. I would like to present the book as a circle. In Figure 1, I present this in a diagram.

Since the chapters are connected, there is some duplication of ideas. I try to avoid repetition, and first give a general introduction, in this chapter, of basic ideas that return in some form, and later a more detailed development of those ideas.

As said, the central chapter is the fourth, on the individual and society, followed by a chapter on morality and ethics. The other three chapters are preparatory. Since I take a process view of the individual and society, I begin with evolution, then consider knowledge in its dynamic aspect of learning, then language and the change of meaning, which I relate to a logic of learning. A fruitful model of change is that of evolution and I will start with that, in Chapter 1. I later apply evolutionary logic to the development of knowledge, in Chapter 2, of language, in Chapter 3, of the human being and society, in Chapter 4, and of morality and ethics, in Chapter 5.

A field related to the logic of evolution is that of learning, in Chapter 2. How do we know whether, in what sense, and in what way, our conceptualisation of the world is adequate? The pragmatic view is that it should matter for action, serve a practical purpose. Whether it correctly represents reality,

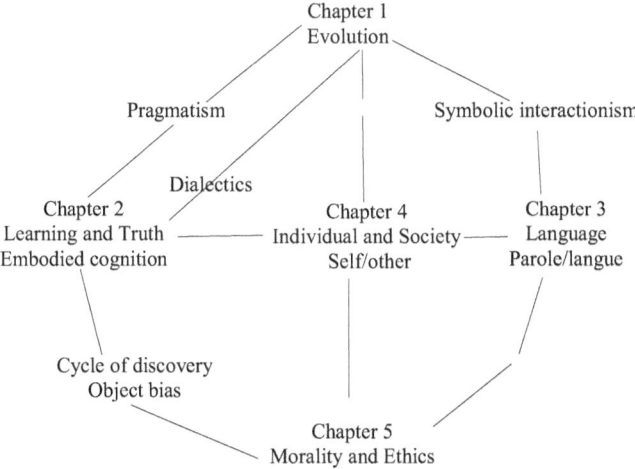

Figure 1. Design of the book

we don't know, since we cannot descend from our ideas to step into the world. But when it fails, we may find out. This is Karl Popper's (1959) principle of falsification. That is not straightforward, since it is based on facts, and there can be misunderstanding and bias concerning facts, since they can depend on different views from the different theoretical perspectives that are up for the test (Kuhn 1970). Still, this is often exaggerated: often facts are not problematic and can be agreed upon, when different interpretations and constructions of facts are not connected to differences in theory, but rest on a deeper, more fundamental theory that is shared.

Another issue is art. How can it be characterized, and what is its function in life, if any? On this issue I have a few things to say, but I must be more modest: I am not sure, and I don't master all the relevant literature.

As an issue in itself, as well as across all other issues, there is the issue of language, discussed in Chapter 3. How adequate is it, what roles does it play in the development and functioning of the human being, in the relation between individual and society, in knowledge, morality and art? What is meaning and how does it change?

A key question is whether and how in realising itself, a potential can produce a new potential or capacity. For that I use Jean Piaget's notion of how perception is 'assimilated' in existing mental frames, constructed in the past and adapting to current phenomena, in 'accommodation' when that fails. The latter reflects Hegel's saying that we get to know things in their failure.

I employ insights from sociology, linguistics and epistemology. I try to configure the jigsaw puzzle, including some pieces of my own previous research. In picking up bits and pieces from a variety of philosophers, I cannot treat them in the detail that those ideas and thinkers would merit, and that scholarly analysis may demand. It is up to the specialists to judge whether what I say is warranted. I opt for survey and coherence, being a bird rather than a mole. Sometimes, what I learned most recently gets more attention than what I learned earlier, which has sunk deeper into me, to the point that the source sometimes becomes irretrievable.

Process Philosophy

My process view is that everything is movement. A material object is made up of molecules, made up from electrons and a nucleus of neutrons and protons, made up from quarks, made up from still only partially understood waves, which all move. Colour is the wavelength of reflected light. The view of an object as a static entity, with a fixed identity, derives from the coherence of its components in a whole that 'emerges' from them with properties that the parts do not have, so that it cannot be split up without losing its identity. It has the potential to affect and be affected, to a greater or lesser extent, by other objects. Yet, objects are events, in the change of their composition of elements, and of the elements themselves, but when that change is slow relative to that of the object's environment, or our observation and experience of that environment, it is seen as a static thing, often to the neglect of its change except from its change of location in space.

A puzzle is that, after the new insights from physics, some scientists claim that time does not exist – it is an illusion (Buonomano 2017). I cannot understand or accept that, in view of another part of physics: the second law of thermodynamics, according to which entropy, disorder, with more and more even and less connected components, increases in systems that are closed, no longer interacting with their environment, which implies the arrow of time. It cannot go in the other direction. A scrambled egg cannot unscramble itself.

Henri Bergson was a prominent process philosopher, and has been a source of inspiration to me, though I fundamentally disagree with parts of his philosophy. I agree that experience and phenomena are not like a series of disconnected points, but like a continuous line, a process, which he called 'duration'. Not a drum but a violin. However, there are accelerations and pauses; consolidation and break-up; expansion and contraction; interaction and separation; poise, equilibration and deviation; fragmentation and integration; ebb and flow. A melody moves across pauses. Things can pulsate and throb. A wave has amplitude and frequency. The French philosopher Gaston

Bachelard (1950) wrote of 'the dialectic of duration' and 'rhythm'. All this applies metaphysically, by assumption, to things, and is experienced in thought and listening to a melody. A dynamic equilibrium is composed of change. In linguistic terms, the focus is not on subject and object and their attributes, but on the verb of its being, in interaction. This aligns with pragmatism. In sum, duration is continuous but not regular.

I further employ ideas from evolution theory, Nietzsche's 'Dionysian' creative destruction, social interactionism (Mead 2011), Kierkegaard's existentialism, Heidegger's 'being in the world' ('Dasein'), meaning as use (Wittgenstein), and Saussure's notion of the living dynamic of the meanings of words in use ('parole') as opposed to their static intersubjective order ('langue').

Another process philosopher was Gilles Deleuze. He distinguished between the external difference of a thing with respect to other things and its internal differentiation, which he saw as a process of development, akin to Bergson's 'duration'. I agree with Deleuze that philosophy should not remain stuck in criticism and should engage in ongoing new ideas, aimed, here also, as in pragmatism, at solving ever new problems. But, to my surprise, Deleuze argues against criticism and dialogue. For me, philosophy should offer 'creative destruction', on the basis of criticism and debate, creation arising from criticism. The best resource one has, to correct one's misconceptions, is difference of opinion. I share Deleuze's fascination with Nietzsche's Dionysian vitalism. However, this is presented by Nietzsche as an almost solipsistic affair, arising from the autonomous, creative self, in affirmation, not negation. However, in my view creation arises out of contrast and diversity, in opposition, and I affirm a Hegelian dialectic, where one gets to know something in its limitation and failure. This dialectic is not the realisation of something inevitable, as claimed by some, as the necessary realisation of an Hegelian absolute spirit. And I doubt that Hegel intended it that way.

Affirmation of the self is a kind of intellectual incest. Deleuze recognises the need for diversity, and mutual influence of philosophy, science and art, and I don't see how that could work without mutual complementation that implies opposition and criticism. Also, I don't see how lack of criticism and opposition can go together with Nietzschean will to power.

The human being has a drive to distinguish itself, to satisfy its drive to live, in 'thymos', self-manifestation. Thymos, I think, is the Dionysian drive in life, propounded by Nietzsche, next to the Apollonian striving towards harmony and balance. Spinoza recognised 'conatus' as the drive to live, apparently similar to thymos. Plato gave the metaphor of reason as a charioteer, holding in check two wild horses of eros and thymos. I think those are not necessarily bad, and should not be brought to a standstill. Thymos is found among entrepreneurs, and scholars or scientists, who wish to engage in the challenge of realising their ideas, often to the benefit of society. A Nietzschean drive to power, in the sense of affecting the choice of others is self-defeating. One should let oneself be affected by others. Thymos is related to Bandura's concept of 'self-efficacy', people's beliefs that 'influence aspirations and the outcome they expect for their effort, what courses of action to pursue, how much effort will people invest? How long will they persevere in the face of obstacles and failure, their resilience after setbacks' (Smith and Bond 1993, 84)?

Critical communication never is only the absorption of new ideas in an existing frame, but always the shift of the frame, in a new constellation, and that is part of the interchange between people. Affirmation of the individual, asserting its individual life force, happens in combination with, and partly as a result of, interactive criticism.

Also, Deleuze goes along with Nietzsche's principle of eternal return. That return may be true, in an eternal cycle of an expanding and contracting universe, in boom and bust, as claimed by some cosmologists, but that is not what Nietzsche means. What he means is a plea to live fully, with the necessary courage to face what one cannot control, and commitment to whatever happens, as if you would want it again and again, in a love of fate, but I find it difficult to see how the notion of eternal return can be reconciled with Dionysian dynamics, where in my view nothing, except perhaps the principles of dynamics itself, ever returns, in ongoing change.

Change is not real, according to Plato. It was impossible according to Parmenides, because creation out of nothing is impossible, and if something arises out of something it is not really new. Aristotle solved this issue with his notion of entelechy, inherent potential to develop something, and realising that potential, like an oak growing out of an acorn.

In philosophy there has been a stream, with Derrida and Deleuze, for example, against what was called the 'philosophy of presentation', seen as an obsession with what is given, a static present, a 'thing'. I agree that the present does not exist, as a dot in time, in that it is ephemeral, continually dissolving into the past. All that exists is the Bergsonian flow of time, change.

Oger raised the question whether Derrida escapes from teleology, with a given goal one strives for, the problem one aims to solve, as pragmatism would have it. I think the answer is simple. The goal is never given fully, unambiguously and fixed. It shifts as one moves towards it. It is often in action that one constructs or reconstructs a goal, which then moves on in further adaptation. The horizon recedes. A problem turns out to be different from what one thought before, and I think this is in line with Derrida's thought.

This connects with a debate in economics. The standard approach of economic theory is that action aims at something efficiently, with a minimum use of scarce resources, on the basis of given 'preferences'. But the preferences form in action. They are, or should be, *endogenous*, something to be explained, not assumed. Hayek characterised competition in markets as a 'discovery process', and that is what makes markets effective, in discovering what one can best produce, and adapt in ongoing competition. In the business literature, this has yielded the notion of 'dynamic capabilities', to go beyond the effective and efficient usage of existing resources, in the discovery or development of new ones. I will return to that later.

Bergson (1969) went so far as to say that 'there is change but there are no things that change'. That is the case, I think, but in some things the change is slow compared to that in the thing's environment, or occurs in the underlying buzz of elementary particles and quantum waves. That is unobservable. So, for many practical purposes, I do not know how to think without a notion of things as more or less stable. I recall that Bergson said that when two trains run in parallel at the same speed, people in the trains are static with respect to each other. A thing is composed of other things that also are processes of change. The identity of a body is maintained by keeping the change of its components and their composition within limits, in the salinity and acidity and temperature of the body, for example.

The process view of life links with the definition of life as resisting the natural law (the second law of thermodynamics) of entropy maximisation in closed systems, that is, the dissipation of any organisation of matter, by maintaining an openness of the system, processing an intake of food, producing energy, excreting refuse and fighting aggressive infections – maintaining an equilibrium of life processes. The process view also connects with Kierkegaard's existential view of life as finding one's path with choices, decisions and acts.

An exemplary view of change is that of evolution, the subject of the next chapter.

Chapter 1

EVOLUTION

An evolutionary approach is useful because it contributes to the explanation of the origin and development of the human being and society without prior 'intelligent design', and also clarifies the potential for their development, as well as its limitations. This applies to all areas of investigation in this book: knowledge, language, agency of the human being and morals/ethics.

As widely known, the logic of evolution is that of the threesome of variety generation, selection and transmission. In biology, variety generation takes the form of mutation of genes and conditions for their expression, and in sexual reproduction the cross-over of chromosomes. Lamarck held that characteristics acquired during life can be transmitted in reproduction. That idea was dropped because it is not clear how such experience could be incorporated in genes. However, it was later seen that genes often do not directly entail characteristics themselves, but a potential to produce them, in 'gene expression', as a function of the environment, in which experience does play a direct role. The colour of eyes is an exception, as determined more directly by genes.

That matters especially because in contrast with most animals, humans are born long before maturity, with further development in the environment in which they are born and brought up. That came about when the precursor of the human being started to stand and walk upright, which narrowed the pelvis as exit for the baby, while the human being also increased the size of its brain and with that the size of its skull, further blocking the baby's exit, necessitating early birth. The early birth makes for vulnerability and, as a result, the need for baby care. The growth of the brain, in turn, enabled the wider use of now freed hands, for tool use, and larger mental capacity for social interaction that was needed, among other things, for division of labour in child care, which in turn favoured a larger brain. That early birth makes for malleability, and social cooperation, which increases the potential for survival.

Universal Darwinism

Beyond biology, a generalised evolutionary theory, with its basic principles of *variety generation, selection and transmission,* has been applied to a wide range of socioeconomic phenomena, such as organisations (Aldrich 1999; Baum and Singh 1994; McKelvey 1982), industries (Hannan and Freeman 1977, 1984, 1989), economies (Hodgson 1998, 2002b; Hodgson and Knudsen 2004; Metcalfe 1998; Nelson and Winter 1982; Veblen 2009; Witt 2004), knowledge (Campbell 1974), neural structures (Edelman 1987) and culture (Boyd and Richerson 1985; Hull 1988).

In behavioural science, the evolutionary perspective has a number of attractions. It explains development and spread of forms of organisation, culture, meanings and cognition under limited foresight, and hence limited planning. In economics and management, evolutionary theory keeps us from the error of an unrealistically rational, magical view of development as the design by somehow prescient, or even clairvoyant, managers, entrepreneurs and scientists, as well as from the opposite error of institutional or technological determinism, whereby forms of organisation are dictated by external conditions of technology and market (McKelvey 1982). In the first, managerial actors are omnipotent, and in the latter actors are absent. Evolutionary theory helps to deal with what in sociology is called the problem of agency and structure, how structure constrains and enables agency, but is also produced by it. It forces us to recognise both the role of actors, with their individual preferences and endowments, in the processes of variety generation and transmission, and the enabling and constraining conditions for action, in structures of markets and institutions, in the process of selection. While characteristics of entrepreneurs and organisations have a causal effect on survival and growth of firms, causality can also go another way, with those characteristics being the result of processes of selection and retention (Aldrich 1999, 336). It forces us to recognise causes of change both within organisations ('autogenic') and outside them ('allogenic') (McKelvey 1982). It makes allowance for the radical uncertainty of innovation (Shackle 1961), and for evident and ubiquitous error and failure in human endeavour.

Of great intellectual but also moral importance, evolutionary theory also forces us to accept diversity as an essential element of societies and their development. The old practice, in economic analysis, of dealing with an industry on the basis of a 'representative firm' is a fundamental mistake. As Hayek recognised, knowledge is dispersed and differentiated.

Competition in markets and fields of knowledge, with constraining and enabling effects of institutions, is straightforwardly seen as yielding a process of differential survival and retention of products, practices and ideas. There is plausibility in seeing entrepreneurship and invention as sources of variety generation, and to see personnel turnover, training, personnel transfer, imitation, consultancy and growth as mechanisms for the transmission of proven success.

However, anyone who has studied socioeconomic evolution recognises that in many respects it differs radically from biological evolution. Evolution requires some stability of the selection environment for selection to work, while the system of an economy seems to be in perpetual shift, due to political change, rapid innovation and economies of scale that yield concentration and lobbying power. While earlier literature was often based on analogies from biological evolution, in more recent literature (Hodgson 2002b; Hodgson and Knudsen 2004, 2006) a radical abstraction has been made, in the definition of 'universal Darwinism' (Dawkins 1983) in terms of only the overall 'meta-theoretical framework' (Hodgson and Knudsen 2006, 16) of *variety generation, selection and transmission*, regardless of the very different ways in which those operate in different areas of application. Hodgson and Knudsen claim that this overall framework applies universally to biological as well as economic, cultural and cognitive systems. It is needed to explain why some organisations last longer or grow more than others, and why some are imitated more than others (Hodgson and Knudsen 2004). While universal Darwinism gives a useful conceptual orientation of research, in not assuming rational design, it leaves most of the explanatory work still to be done, in a specification of the processes of variety generation, selection and transmission, in terms of people, cognition, work, management, science, invention, innovation, organisations, industries, markets and institutions.

Universal Darwinism specifies the principles of variety generation, selection and transmission in terms of the notions of *replicators* and *interactors* (Campbell 1974; Hull 1988; McKelvey 1982) or *vehicles* (Dawkins 1983), and the notion of *populations*. Interactors/vehicles (in biology: organisms) interact with their selection environment, and are members of *populations* of similar but differentiated interactors (in biology: species). The suggestion is that these are essential elements of evolution, without which the notion of evolution becomes loose and indeterminate. They distinguish Darwinism from a more general, looser, less determinate notion of evolution in the sense of 'development'. However, as argued recently by Nelson (2006), this is also where the problems begin. The question then is how meaningful evolutionary theory is as the notions of interactors and replicators turn out to fail to apply. As discussed below, to function as an interactor, an entity must have a reasonably cohesive and stable set of components. This is the *ecological* side of evolution (Baum and Singh 1994). Interactors carry replicators (in biology: genes) that in the *ontogenetic* development of interactors generate characteristics that affect their survival and thereby the replication of their replicators. This generation of characteristics (in biology: gene expression) takes place in interaction, within the interactor, between replicators and other features of the interactor, as well as with the environment of the interactor. Replicators may lie dormant, yielding a potential, until triggered by conditions. Note that it is not the replicators themselves that determine survival but the characteristics that they produce. Replicators may generate characteristics on different levels, including abilities to generate characteristics, depending on the circumstances. Replicators from surviving interactors are replicated and re-combined, mostly within populations of interactors that partake of a common pool of replicators. This is the *genealogical* side of evolution, in the *phylogenetics* of a species.

In economics, firms, in particular, are seen as interactors in their environments of markets and institutions in which they may go bankrupt, and are members of industries that are seen as populations, and their competencies (McKelvey 1982) or behavioural routines (Nelson and Winter 1982) are seen as the corresponding replicators, with industries sharing a common pool of such competencies. In a *lineage* of firms, those are similar by transmission or imitation.

In science, interactors, presumably, are scientists, with survival here denoting career success, and their replicators are basic ideas, perhaps making up the 'core' of a 'scientific research programme'(Lakatos 1978, see later). A lineage then is a sequence of theories in that research programme, adopting the same theoretical 'core' (Lakatos), and adding to the 'protective belt' that operationalises the core.

There are several limitations in the application of Darwinian evolution to economics and culture. In the economy there are issues of information. Survival of firms depends on their ability to access and absorb information, about markets, technology and institutions. Here, there is economy of scale: the cost of a bit of information depends on its acquisition, not on its use and size of the firm, so that in a large firm the costs are relatively lower. There does not seem to be anything similar in biological evolution. (Rosenberg 2000). Acquired information is transmitted, which would make evolution Lamarckian. A complication lies in what is called 'co-evolution', where the units to be selected can affect the selection environment, to enhance survival, in 'niche construction' (Aldrich 1999). Examples in biology are birds building nests, rabbits digging warrens, beavers constructing dams. There are also several forms of parasitism and symbiosis, such as small fish cleaning the teeth in the maw of a shark. In economies, there is an increase of scale and concentration of firms that reduce competition in markets, innovation that constructs new markets and shifts old ones, and protective lobbying that avoids selection by markets and institutions. In politics, there is political manipulation, rhetoric, censorship or other forms of suppression or evasion of criticism and competition. When such co-evolution goes too far, selection is no longer effective and evolution breaks down.

In the following, I elaborate on the three least researched aspects of evolution in social science (Baum and Singh 1994): the identity of interactors, the nature and characteristics of replication and the process of variety generation. I give a discussion of key issues in social science, in order to specify the questions. I summarise a theory of cognition used here, and the cognitive view of organisations to which it leads, as discussed in Nooteboom (2000, 2006, 2009), discussed in Chapter 2. This yields a view on the possible nature of the replicators, the identity of organisations as interactors, and on intra- and inter-population differences between them.

Third, I give an analysis of the sources of variation. In the literature on organisations, the present discussion falls squarely in what Aldrich (1999) called the 'knowledge development' stream of organisation theory. Here, use of insights from cognitive science is inspired by the fact that in socioeconomics both replication and variety generation are fundamentally cognitive and linguistic processes (Nooteboom 2000).

Interactors and Replicators

How is a replicator replicated, and why is there increasing complexity of things in evolution? In nature and culture there are *complex adaptive systems* (CAS) that arise, often spontaneously, in self-organisation, where component systems combine in a higher-level system with new functions. The DNA wrapped up in a cell guides how the cell combines with other cells, under local conditions, in the configuration of an organ. There was increasing complexity in a configuration of specialised organs because specialisation of function enhances efficiency, that is, lesser use of resources, and increases the scope of response to a changing selection environment, and hence increases the chances of survival.

The literature on evolutionary theory of organisations allows for connected evolutionary processes on multiple levels: of skills and jobs; of workgroups or *communities of practice* (Brown and Duguid 1996) within organisations (Burgelman 1983); of organisations within industries; and of industries in wider socioeconomic systems (Baum and Singh 1994). However, it is not always clear what, precisely, the interactors and replicators are, on different levels. Here I focus on organisations as interactors in industries, and on scholars as interactors in disciplines or scholarly 'fora' (de Groot 1969). The following questions arise.

The most fundamental question is to what extent in socioeconomics the notions of interactors and replicators make sense at all (cf. Nelson 2006).

Unlike biology, the evolution of interactors, in the form of organisations, and replicators, in the form of organisational competencies, routines and scientific ideas, does not depend on the survival of the interactors that carry them, as noted, for example, by Nelson (2006). It is not even completely clear what 'failure' or 'being selected out' entails, and I will return to this point later. Whatever it means, competencies and ideas from organisations and scholars may be adopted by other organisations and scholars long after the latter have 'failed'. Often geniuses are not recognised, and their ideas are not adopted, until long after their death. Ideas can subside into obscurity, lurking in libraries, to be rediscovered or re-evaluated much later, without the need for intervening survival of its carrier. When organisations or scholars fail, whatever that means, some of their capabilities or ideas may still be seen as useful and adopted accordingly. Thus, purported replicators may float around, so to speak, disembodied from their carriers, possibly buried in unpublished documents, before they are replicated. If replicators may be disembodied from interactors, does the notion still make sense?

In biology, replicators generate, in ontogenesis, the interactors that carry them. As noted before, in biology but to a greater extent in organisation and scholarship, actors not only are active in interacting with their environment but also engage in cognitive construction, which entails that they develop their replicators on the basis of experience (Witt 2005). As is widely recognised, ontogenetically produced replicators may be adopted by others, so that here evolution is, at least in part, Lamarckian, with 'inheritance of acquired characteristics'. Thus, while interactors may be generated by replicators they also generate them. Furthermore, according to the perspective of *embodied cognition*, to be discussed later, interactors develop in interaction with a variety of other people, adopting and transforming some of their ideas and skills. Thus they are generated by the replicators not only of any well-defined parent, but from a host of other interactors with greater or lesser 'parenthood'. The notions of 'parents' and 'offspring' become diffuse. While in biology there is a clear separation between ontogenetic and phylogenetic development, in society there is not (Witt 2005).

If in society, in economics and science, interactors shape their replicators, then a key question is how far such shaping goes, and to what extent it reliably reflects selection conditions. Hodgson and Knudsen (2004, 2006) recognise that if direct shaping of replicators by their carriers were complete and fast, and would reliably reflect any shift or variety of the selection environment, evolution would break down. Survival would no longer be an indicator of success, and many unproven, worthless or deleterious traits would be imitated along with favourable ones. In other words, as recognised by most authors, for evolution to work there must be some isolation of replicators from influence by interactors, or, in other words, some inertia of interactors (Hannan and Freeman 1984). My worry here is that the shaping of replicators may indeed to a considerable extent reflect often more or less erroneously perceived or inferred changes in the selection environment, in ways unproven by selection, and that indeed 'many unproven, worthless or deleterious traits (are) imitated along with favorable ones'. Here, Darwinism does indeed break down. In financial markets excessive risk-taking took a long time before producing a financial crisis, and banks failing to fail were propped up by governments because they were 'too big to fail'.

For groups of people, such as organisations, to operate as interactors, in evolutionary terms there must be group selection. For that to work, individual interests must somehow be subjugated, to a sufficient extent, to collective interest. Organisational identity, cohesiveness and stability may be prevented by the dominance of centrifugal individual or group interests within the firm (Campbell 1974). So, what provides organisational cohesion and stability? Is there some durable identity?

In the evolution of science, scholarly societies are also organisations, and a similar question arises there: If scholars are interactors, what are their replicators? The meaning of the notion of 'replicator' has several dimensions: (1) things that are carried by an interactor, (2) things that generate the interactor's characteristics relevant for success or failure in its interaction with its selection environment, and (3) things that are transmitted to generate new interactors.

Organisation has been seen as a system for 'sense-making' (Weick 1995), 'collective mind' (Weick and Roberts 1993) and system of 'shared meanings' (Smircich 1983). McKelvey (1982) proposed that organisations are characterised by 'dominant competencies'. Nelson and Winter (1982) used the term 'routines', but there is some ambiguity and confusion around that term, and I prefer McKelvey's terminology. What, precisely, are these? In earlier work (Nooteboom 2000, 2006, 2009) I proposed that organisations require an organisational 'cognitive focus' to limit 'cognitive distance' between people inside organisations, in order to achieve effective exploitation of resources. Here I propose that such focus yields an organisational identity that has some stability.

Organisational focus enables but also constrains absorption of novelty that feeds organisational change. It functions as a filter for admitting and accepting outside ideas and people. In other words, organisations are indeed subject to greater or lesser 'inertia' (Hannan and Freeman 1989). However, it remains to be seen to what extent organisations may escape from inertia. Indeed, the very notion of 'radical innovation' seems to entail such an escape. I will discuss organisational focus in more detail later.

In scholarly societies, established paradigms to some extent encapsulate that society from its environment. Are scholars interactors, or their theories? If scholars are interactors, are their replicators ideas, hypotheses or theories? If theories are interactors, what are their replicators? Key ideas or paradigms, perhaps. These theories or ideas can indeed be seen as being carried by scholars to generate their cognitive identities, and to be subject to transmission to others. However, as already noted, those replicators may also be transmitted as disembodied from their carriers, to adopters whose identities are composed from multiple sources.

To what extent can we meaningfully speak of 'replication' at all? Replication entails the maintenance of the content, properties of a replicator, with only occasional or limited 'copying errors', and without significant transformation of form, content or function. Is transmission of organisational competencies and ideas, and of ideas in science, sufficiently like that? In my view (cf. Nooteboom 2000), in communication significant transformation of meaning generally occurs, in the process of absorption or assimilation into existing mental frames. Such assimilation is not a passive act of copying but an active process of structuration and transformation.

For industries to make sense as populations of organisations, there must be both differences and similarities between firms within an industry, and possibilities for replication that are greater within than between industries. Due to imitation and personnel mobility between organisations in an industry, or even between industries, organisational identities may not be sufficiently differentiated and isolated for selection to work (Boyd and Richerson 1985). How do we account for intra- and inter-industry differentiation?

In science, do disciplines make sense as populations? Or are the populations here scientific societies within or across disciplines, or are those to be seen as niches within disciplines?

In sum, the questions in this section are, among others, the following: What constitutes the replicators of organisations, in the form of organisation-level competencies? How do these yield a cohesive and stable organisational identity? How does this yield differences as well as similarities within industries, more opportunities for replication within than between industries, and some but limited shaping of competencies as a function of experience in environments of markets and institutions? Partial answers have already been given. In the following I will analyse the questions in more detail.

Selection

In socioeconomics, what is failure of interactors under selection? Is it the death of the interactor (organisation, scholar), or some other manifestation of failure? In the context of firms selection arises from competition in markets, which may lead to their bankruptcy, take-over, break-up or management buy-out. As noted earlier, even in case of complete failure, in bankruptcy, some of its capabilities may be adopted as useful by others.

In science, selection takes the form of refutation, ideally on the basis of empirical falsification (Popper 1959), or critical debate in scientific 'fora', rejection of papers by journals and rejection of proposals by funding agencies. This may kill but only one idea or publication, which may subsequently be revised or improved to survive later in a different form.

Also, as noted by Witt (2005) and Nelson (2006), particularly in economics as well as in science, there is much 'pre-practice' testing – in mental thought experiments, debate, computer simulations, the testing of prototypes, market testing and consumer 'focus groups'. Human beings learn such testing and experimentation before practice at an early age, in child's play and sports, and proceed to refine their mental experimentation in later education. Such pre-practice testing would have to be included in the notion of selection. However, that means that some selection is not in the selection 'environment' but internal to an individual person or organisation.

As noted before, a key issue in evolutionary theory of organisations and scholarship is that singly or collectively they can to a greater or lesser extent affect or even mould the external selection environment of markets and institutions to favour their survival and reproduction, in *co-evolution*. Selection is political, and is shaped or avoided by debate, rhetoric, indoctrination, coalition formation and positions of power and influence (or the lack of it). Are these to be seen as part of selection or as avoidance of it? While influence of interactors on the selection environment, in co-evolution, is not unique for socioeconomics, and also occurs to a considerable extent in biology, in economic systems the scope for it seems to be of a different order of magnitude, on the basis of intelligent inference of selection forces and the ability, power and political influence of some organisations to shape such forces, in setting standards of technology, conditions of legitimacy, shaping market structure (e.g. distribution channels) and erecting entry barriers.

An example of the setting of selection conditions from Garud and Rappa (1996) concerns the rivalry between two competing technologies for hearing aids in the form of implants in the cochlea, in the inner ear. There were two rival systems: a single-channel and a multiple-channel device. The first carried less risk than the second did, but the second yielded a greater and easier improvement of hearing. The problem was that objective, independent evaluation of these dimensions of performance were not available, and the choice between them is subjective. The same ideas that informed the choice of device also informed the methodologies for selecting between them, so that there were rival evaluation methods. The rival methods were championed by rival commercial interest groups, and the stakes were high. The single-channel group argued that the obvious choice was to begin with this low-risk device, and step up to the other after its risks were clearer and could be reduced. The multiple-channel group argued that this would not reduce risk but add to it in the process of taking out one device and replacing it with the other. No objective experience was available to back up either claim.

Let me give another illustration. In the innovation of a cotton carpet (instead of wool), it was first introduced for bedrooms, in view of the moisture-regulating properties of cotton and its nice feel to bare feet. However, cotton fibre does not have the natural resilience of wool, so that in its use the pile of a cotton carpet rapidly flattens, but after vacuuming regains its fresh look. Now, resistance of carpets to such pile flattening was a key feature in the existing certification of quality, thus favouring wool over cotton, and the new carpet could effectively enter the market only after the innovator, sufficiently large and influential, managed to wield his influence to have the certification procedure modified to accept vacuuming prior to inspection. Such actions to mould the selection environment are also amply illustrated by Aldrich (1999, 334).

In science, when scholars face a lack of survival and replication of their ideas, in failed access to journals, or in their papers remaining ignored or uncited, they can, and often do, create their own selection environment by founding their own scholarly societies with more or less proprietary journals. Also, their ideas survive not only, and perhaps not even primarily, from scientific as much as from organisational and rhetorical skills.

One may argue, however, that even though for these reasons selection may be limited or inefficient, not even the most visionary entrepreneur or scientist, nor the most powerful of corporations, nor the most able organiser or rhetorician can completely mould his environment to guarantee success, survival and dominance, and some selective pressure will remain. The limits of co-evolution are not only limits of power, but also cognitive limits. One is not infallible in inferring what structure of selection favours differential survival and growth, for lack of insight in causalities of selection and in opportunities that any change might yield to unforeseeable new innovations that may constitute a threat to incumbent organisations.

Returning to the example of the cotton carpet, the most salient thing is perhaps that it took effort to alter the selection conditions, even in only one though crucial respect, which might have failed, in which case the innovation would likely not have survived. While there is much more to be said about this issue, it is not a subject for the present book, since although selection seems very imperfect it still may be adequate enough to let this issue pass. In sum, for the sake of argument here I will accept that selection by competition still makes sufficient sense, in markets and scientific rivalry.

Replication

A third issue concerns processes of replication, and the relation between replication and variety generation. In socioeconomic evolution, replication entails reproduction and imitation of knowledge and competencies. This occurs on the basis of observation, communication and apprenticeship. Successful products and practices are copied or imitated on the basis of observation and inference, reverse engineering, publications and documents, oral presentations, courses, reports, explanations by consultants and the like.

Apprenticeship may merit special notice. Knowledge is externalised not only in speech, documents, software, ostensive activity or role models, but is also embodied in tools, in a general sense, including machines, procedures and forms of organisation. In learning to use tools, an apprentice may reconstruct some of the mental schema's that lay behind the design and production of the tool. In socioeconomics, these forms of replication entail linguistic processes of expression, and cognitive processes of assimilation into mental *schemata* (Aldrich 1999; Piaget 1970, 1974) or *mental models* (Johnson-Laird 1983) that constitute *absorptive capacity* (Cohen and Levinthal 1990). This is fundamentally different from replication of genes in biology. Replication of knowledge and competencies is

- at least partly voluntary and subject to choice: one adopts what is perceived to be successful.
- partial: one may, within restrictions of systemic coherence, adopt only part of a bundle of replicators carried by a given interactor.
- subject to decay, distortion, reduction, extension and transformation, going far beyond the copying errors, deletions and duplications of genes in biology.

In other words, replication at the same time entails a kind of variety generation.

In Chapter 2 on learning and truth this issue will be analysed The role of language and the change of meaning will be taken up in Chapter 3.

Variation

A fourth issue, in evolutionary theory, concerns the sources of variation, in particular the question how blind and how independent from selection variety generation is. According to most evolutionary accounts, the main trigger of radical innovation is a shock in the form of a break or shift of the selection environment, which may renew the pressure of competition for scarce resources, disadvantage incumbent species and create new opportunities for new variety. Such a shift or shock may be due to natural disaster, a pandemic like Corona, political upheaval and war, a shift in demand, a shift in institutions (e.g. regulations for protecting the environment) or a shift due to developments in related industries or markets. However, this tells us only of new opportunities, not of how they arise and are exploited.

In evolutionary theory as applied to nature, generation of new variety, in new interpretations or new ideas, is generally ascribed to errors in replication, and random, uninformed trials as steps into the dark ('mutations'). In the methodology of CAS (Holland, 1996), the conduct of agents is modelled in terms of if-then rules, which are sometimes modelled, in analogy to chromosomes, as bit-strings of messages sent in response to bit-strings of messages received, and the discovery of rules is modelled as random mutations of values at positions in the string plus random crossover of strings, in analogy to sexual reproduction. How valid or adequate is this, as a model of human learning and communication?

In socioeconomic evolution there is much trial and error in entrepreneurial venturing, and more so to the extent that the innovation is radical, that is, entails destruction of existing competencies (Anderson and Tushman 1990; Tushman and Anderson 1986), technologies, and forms of organisation, limiting the opportunity to build on existing knowledge and competence. However, evidently in socioeconomic evolution there is invention and knowledge development that is informed, somehow, by experience from failures and resulting inferences about where sources of failure may lie and where to look for improvements. This is too obvious to ignore or deny, and Aldrich (1999), Foster and Metcalfe (2001) and Nelson and Winter (1982), to name only a few, all recognised that next to blindness there is also intentional, deliberate and somehow directed variety generation. Thus, according to Foster and Metcalfe (2001, 10) 'the rate of economic progress that we observe reflects guided variation within conceptual schemes that channel explorative, creative enquiry in particular directions'. They add: 'Of course, all variation is, in effect, blind variation, since it necessarily deals with the unknowable consequences of a present decision.' However, if the search is guided by inference, while that does not spell out consequences, I would not call it blind. What does it mean that variation is 'both guided and blind'? Little, if anything, in the evolutionary literature, is said of how the 'guidance' or 'direction' of variation works in 'explorative, creative enquiry'. More generally, the generation of variety is the least developed side of evolution in socioeconomic systems (Baum and Singh 1994, 18). According to Hodgson and Knudsen (2004 11) evolution is blind in two senses. First, 'particular outcomes are not necessarily prefigured or predicted in advance'. I agree with that. However, this leaves open the possibility of an intelligent design of a heuristic path, a logic of discovery, guided by experience, which is likely to yield radical novelty, even though it cannot be predicted what that will be. That is precisely what I will argue, with a 'cycle of discovery', in Chapter 2 on learning.

According to Campbell (1987), 'any capacity for foresight or prescience must be based on tried and tested knowledge, otherwise we have no grounds to presume its effectiveness'. Accordingly, when genuine innovations are launched, we are unable to assess the probability of their success or failure (Hodgson and Knudsen 2006, 11). I agree with the first part (experience is needed to presume effectiveness), but I disagree with the second part. Because we can make inferences from experience we can 'presume effectiveness', that is, increased likelihood of success beyond blind trials, even if perhaps that cannot be rendered in terms of probability theory (cf. Shackle 1961), but in terms of the analysis of scenarios.

Campbell (1987 specified blindness as entailing variations that are (1) independent of each other, (2) separate from the environment, (3) uncorrelated with the solution and (4) later variations are not corrections of former ones. Applying these criteria, in the next chapter I will argue that there is non-blind variation.

In Sum

When evolution is abstracted from biological evolution, in 'Universal Darwinism', with only the bare notions of variety generation, selection and replication, without specification of how those processes work, it can to some extent be made to fit socioeconomic evolution. The attempt to maintain an evolutionary perspective is useful for developing a coherent combination of internal and external causes of change, and of agency and structure, avoiding both an overly rational view of managerial design and a view of environmental determinism without actors. However, with such a bare, abstracted framework, most of the explanatory work still has to be done. A key question is whether a further elaboration of the framework in terms of interactors and replicators can meaningfully be sustained, and here my doubts are more severe. To the extent that this is a requirement for universal Darwinism, I share the doubts and criticisms of the latter that were voiced before by Witt (2005) and Nelson (2006).

If evolutionary theory is useful but not fully adequate for explaining the evolution of economies, organisations and knowledge, what is the alternative? That is the subject of the following chapters.

Chapter 2

LEARNING AND TRUTH

Philosophy of Science

Let me first say that I am a *realist*, with the claim that there is a real world, even if that world is not completely and perhaps not reliably observed, and science should try to explain it, with the aid of theory. This stands in contrast with *positivism*, which says that we should only deal with what is observed, without theory, which was considered to be metaphysical speculation. This stance is not tenable, and has been superseded, in the philosophy of science, by the view that observation and interpretation are guided by theory, and are thus 'theory laden'. If one claims, in positivism, that the theory is not about 'what exists', and only observation is valid, it becomes a mystery how the theory could 'work', help in dealing with the world. And what about the time that microscopes were not yet there: did microscopic things not exist at the time?

Observation and interpretation not only includes explicit theoretical propositions, but a host of subsidiary or 'background' assumptions, often tacit or taken for granted, about how the world works. The challenge then is to craft implications of the theory that can be observed, to test the theory. Any falsification will again include subsidiary assumptions that one can criticise to disarm the falsification and save the existing theory. Furthermore, the falsifying proposition also is value laden, and hence is not an indisputable fact.

There is the story of the planets Neptune and Vulcan. The planet Neptune appeared to deviate from Newtonian physics, but the apparent anomaly was eliminated with the discovery of the planet Mercury, which could explain the deviation. Another anomaly then concerned Mercury. It was postulated that this anomaly was due to yet another planet called 'Vulcan', which could not be observed, but this could be explained away with the argument that it was so near to the sun that its light was overpowered by that of the sun, but this time that planet was never found, and the anomaly did falsify Newtonian physics, and could be explained by relativity theory.

How can we know whether a theory is true? Karl Popper (1959) proposed that theories cannot be proven but only falsified. Logically, he was right. A theoretical proposition is universal, claiming that under conditions A, B will always happen. No matter how often that is confirmed, up till now, this does not prove that it will be confirmed tomorrow. On the other hand, if it is contradicted by evidence only once, it is falsified. So scientists should seek falsification to make progress.

Also, we still face the 'Kantian' problem that we perceive and interpret the world according to forms of thought that are human and imperfect, so we don't see the world 'as it is in itself'. I would say it a little differently: we don't know that – we don't know to what extent or how our view of the world is biased; we can only speculate about it. According to Imre Lakatos (1978), science takes the form of 'research programmes', collections of theories that have a shared 'hard core' of basic assumptions and methodological principles, and a surrounding 'protective belt' of subsidiary assumptions. When a theory in the programme is falsified, the core is left unaffected, and adjustments are made in the protective belt.

Also, next to the Kantian problem, we cannot 'look in all directions at the same time', talk about everything, so that our knowledge is always partial, incomplete. A familiar objection to Kant's assumptions of fundamental frames of thought is that frames of thought may change. What we see, and how, depends on the construction of frames of perception and interpretation along one's individual life course. That is the predicament of the human being. However, the human being has a mind, with a brain, which inanimate objects do not have. How does it work? How do we invent, construct theories?

There is a claim that a theory of invention would be self-defeating or even self-contradictory, because by definition invention cannot be predicted, is based on confusion between prediction and explanation. One can claim to have some understanding of processes of invention without thereby claiming to be able to predict its outcomes. That applies, for example, to evolutionary theory: it specifies principles of a process without claiming to predict its outcomes.

Going back to David Hume, we find the distinction between fact and value. I want to make the distinction between the ontological and the intentional meaning of it. Since observation is theory-laden, and theory arises from interaction with the world in practices, and practices are inevitably value-laden, observation is also value-laden, so that, ontologically speaking, the distinction fact/value is problematic. However, in having to deal with the world, we still *intend* statements as factual, referential. In communication it matters whether one's counterpart intends it as descriptive or normative. We want to know whether what specialists say about the Corona virus is fact or value. There is a suspicion that the facts they derive, and the rules they derive, in how people should behave, for controlling the virus, are shaped by their limited view and explanation of only medical phenomena.

Let me give another example. Consider the proposition that 'the human being is a social animal'. This is clearly intended as a statement of fact. It goes back to Aristotle, and is based on the norm-driven practice of deliberation in the Athenian democracy. It is value-laden. But one wants to know whether any stated opinion is intended as normative, indicating that people should be social, or claims that is how people are in fact. Similarly, there is debate on whether Machiavelli's talk of the opportunistic, lying, deceiving prince is intended as normative, recommending a practice, or only descriptive of an inconvenient truth, or both.

Constructivism

I adopt the view of 'Interactionism' (Mead 2011), which claims that people perceive, interpret and evaluate the world according to mental categories (or 'frames' or 'mental models') that they have developed, and keep developing, in interaction with their social and physical environment. I also adopt the view of 'embodied cognition', which can be traced to Merleau-Ponty's (1974) view that 'the light of reason is rooted in the dark of the body', and implies a denial of the Cartesian dualism of mind and body. In dualism, the puzzle is how thought can rhyme with matter, and in monism how thought can arise from matter. The idea now is that somehow at some stage of evolution circuits of neurons form thought and awareness of it. To what extent is knowledge explicit and is one aware of it? There is tacit knowledge, in unconscious cognitive routines, which raise the issue of free will.

Let us suppose that indeed the physical structures of the brain generate illusions, about consciousness, free will and knowledge of truth. Even if that were the case, those illusions are real in their consequences as we act upon them, in judgement, speech and other communicative action, the results of which feed back, indeed largely unconsciously, into the physical reality of the brain. Then the two worlds, of ideas and reality, are connected, confronted with each other, in a circle of development in the brain, from ideas to action and interaction, with feedback from action, to construction of the brain. Then reality is embodied in the physical brain.

Damasio (2003) argued that the brain makes webs of neural connections that 'represent', first, on the lowest, unconscious level, internal processes of metabolism, the flows of fluids and neural connections that regulate the body. Next, 'above' the representations of bodily processes, representations are made of phenomena from outside the body, perhaps not so much unlike the old notion of 'association', going back to David Hume. As we go 'higher' up in cognition, at some level there are representations of representations that somehow constitute consciousness.

We learn to deal with things and talk about them before forming a concept of it, and the concept is continually adjusted to practice. 'Model' may be a better term than 'representation', as an isomorphism of action-guided processes, in the form of neural nets of connection. Those models develop in guiding those internal processes, at the same time being formed by them, subconsciously, in a feedback loop. However, in the process we do subconsciously make mental representations in the form of neural circuits. They are not given prior to experience and action, 'ex ante', at least not 'hard-wired', but in a potential to develop ideas, formed in the action, 'ex post', and then drive action until the concept is no longer adequate. I agree with Wittgenstein that words are used as tools, but that does not deny that they are represented in the brain. Language is adopted from teaching and practice, and develops in that practice. It is not an intermediary between thought and the world, but contains the world, so to speak, in forming our views of the world. In pragmatism, the prime evaluator of an idea or expression is its use in practice, as a tool. Any use is not given as the 'true' one, and new uses can develop. A word may be used in ways that do not belong to the uses it arose from or was made for, in metaphor, for example, seeing or using something in terms of something else. A screwdriver may be used as a hammer, to drive in nails. This view of a word as a tool for action derives from Wittgenstein, who is also considered a pragmatist (Malachowsky 2013).

Gerald Edelman (1987) proposed a 'neural Darwinism', as follows. In the brain, ideas take the form of neuronal networks, where the neurons trigger each other's 'firing', more frequently and strongly as the corresponding ideas are 'successful', 'work'. The 'association' between ideas arises from connecting patterns of firing of such networks. The patterns may occur in competition with each other ('Darwinism'). Parallel patterns that occur regularly at the same time get connected, in association. With competition between ideas, as parallel neuronal patterns, we may be said to be 'in two minds' about something.

Since the construction of cognition takes place on the basis of interaction with the physical and social environment, which varies between people, 'different minds think different things', as was recognised by Austrian economists (Lachmann 1978), and there is *cognitive distance* between people to the extent that they have different innate potential and develop their cognition in different environments (Nooteboom 1992, 1999).

This connects with Hayek's (1945) view of localised, distributed and differentiated knowledge, as a result of which markets, with uncoordinated private initiatives, are more efficient than central planning. As a result of context-dependent cognitive structuring, cognition is bounded not only in the sense that one has a limited capacity for rational evaluation, but in the more fundamental sense that one's perspective is biased by experience.

Cognitive distance between people, resulting from variety of experience and innate talent, presents both a problem and an opportunity. The opportunity is that variety of cognition is a source of innovation, in crafting 'novel combinations'. The problem is that to the extent that cognition differs, in cognitive distance, it is more difficult to understand each other and to collaborate and utilise opportunities from cognitive variety. Note that, cognition being a wide concept in this book, cognitive distance entails both difference in intellectual knowledge and difference in feeling and morality, of how people should deal with each other. Cognitive distance yields not only a difficulty of mutual understanding, or limit to *absorptive capacity* (Cohen and Levinthal 1990), but a wider difficulty of collaboration, including a mismatch of moral and motivational aspects of collaboration, often due to cultural difference. In other words, distance includes issues of both competence and governance.

Optimal collaboration requires a trade-off between the upside and the downside of cognitive distance, seeking 'optimal cognitive distance' (Nooteboom 2000; Nooteboom et al. 2007), large enough to offer variety for innovation, and small enough to enable collaboration. Problems arise especially when there are cultural differences, discussed more extensively later. In particular, there are differences between more individualistic and more collectivist countries. There are complications when due to differences in language, but also due to stereotyping, there are differences in habits concerning openness, politeness, sincerity, formality, body language. What greatly helps is experience in dealing with others who think differently, and conversational skills, for example, the use of metaphor, accumulated knowledge, altruism, empathy, sensitivity. The distance can generate not only misunderstanding but also mistrust. Trust is discussed more extensively later. Crossing cultural distance, by a 'boundary spanner' or 'go-between', can produce mistrust of him/her by one's 'home group', a loss of respect and acceptance, in suspicions of being a 'defector' or even 'traitor'.

Entropy

Let us consider the notion of *entropy*. This section is more technical than the others, and readers with little affinity to the subject can skip it. Entropy is the number of alternative compositions of components that a system with given properties can have. If the properties are few or indiscriminate, entropy is large. The mathematical formula for entropy E of a system of n elements i of probability pi is $E = -\sum_{i}^{n} pi.logpi$. For a system of two units of equal probability ½, $E = 1$, called a 'bit'. For a system of four elements of equal probability, $E = 2$ or two bits. For a system with eight elements of equal probability, $E = 3$ or three bits. For a system with n states of equal probability, $E = \log n$. A computational advantage of the log function is that $\log 1/n = -\log n$. E increases with the number of elements n and with their 'evenness', equality of pi, which is their probability of occurrence or prominence or weight or legitimacy. The effect of the number of elements is illustrated above, with n going from two to eight elements. The decrease of E with the 'unevenness' of pi is as follows: For the case with three elements, n with equal $pi = 1/3$, $E = 1.58$ and with $p1 = 2/4$, $p2 = 1/4$, $p3 = 1/4$, $E = 1.5$.

Theil (1967) used the entropy measure as a measure of concentration of sales in markets or production in industries. pi here is the share of seller or producer i. If there is only one seller or producer, there is maximum concentration, $E = 1$, that is, least entropy. The log function $\log n$ increases less than proportionally with n: it increases at a decreasing rate, its derivative being $1/n$. This entails that the increase of entropy slows down. As disorder increases, the resistance to further increase increases. Further increase of 'evenness' becomes more difficult.

A puzzle concerning entropy now is the following. Nature and culture are rife with complex adaptive systems (CAS), systems that are composed from subsystems, such as neutrons, protons and electrons composing atoms; atoms composing molecules; molecules composing organs; organs composing bodies; bees composing colonies; people composing organisations, firms, consumers; institutions composing markets; people and institutions composing nations; nations composing supranational entities like the EU. The puzzle is this. On the one hand, CAS produce order, organisation ('complexity'), and in that sense they decrease entropy. On the other hand, in their development they involve more units, constitute new entities and new functions and thereby increase entropy. How can that be? It depends on their heterogeneity, complementarity. While the subsystems integrate into a new order, they lose autonomy. To create the unity or coherence of the higher system, with its new functions, the subsystems are constrained in their operation, become specialised, losing some functions or narrowing their range, and that constitutes less entropy. In a bee colony, bees are highly specialised as food seekers, gate keepers, soldiers, feeders of the queen bee, (Testa and Kier 2000).

The formula of entropy is incomplete. One should consider not only the number and 'unevenness' of units but also their relations. It is through internal and external relations that identity is constituted, order is created. If relations break down, this is also a feature of decay, of increasing entropy. An incoherent bunch of disconnected entities has more entropy than complementary, interacting ones. In their present breakdown of communities, with dissociated individuals, entropy is increasing. The formula for entropy could be extended as follows:

$$E = - \sum_{i}^{n} pi.logpi. \ |1 - C/M|,$$ where C is the number of direct connections

between units, and M is its optimum, and the vertical slashes indicate absolute value. What is optimal connection depends on the purpose of the system. The maximum number of connections is $n(n - 1)/2$. That is not necessarily optimal, as in an organisation where if all people connect with all, there is noise that distracts from work. If $C = M$, that is, the number of connections is at its optimum, the addition to entropy is 0. If $C = 0$, if there are no connections, the addition is 1. If the number of connections is lower or higher than the optimum, there is addition to entropy. One can picture this as an $n \times n$ matrix with along both axes the n units, and a surface above the matrix that represents the value of interaction for each pair of units. It is likely to have a bulge, at the optimum; some connections have more value than others.

Entropy yields a way of looking at the issue of authenticity and conformism discussed later: people lose some freedom of action for the sake of the coherence of a community or nation. It applies also to language: in the higher order of a sentence, the ambiguity of potential meanings of a word shrinks to a specific meaning determined by the structure and context of the sentence.

In the literature on freedom, a distinction is made between 'negative' freedom, in the absence of external constraint, and 'positive freedom' in access to resources. Here, the subsystem loses negative freedom in constraints imposed or accepted for fitting in the higher system, but gains positive freedom in access to new functions offered by the higher-level system. There is loss of one freedom, and gain of the other.

Politics

In politics, the trade-off between positive and negative freedom is a big issue. Liberalism aims at negative freedom, socialism at positive freedom. Formerly colonised countries are eager to establish a more homogeneous nation and remove the former deviant colonisers, but thereby they lose the resources built up or represented by them. Maalouf (2019) gives examples, such as Egypt under Nasser, in the 1950s, chasing out the English. An exception was Mandela, who did not chase out the former oppressor, and even asked him to stay, in order to contribute to the country.

Increase of entropy, in increase of evenness, can also occur in a non-colonised country. An example is France in 1685, where in an attempt to establish a more homogenous religious society Louis XIV renounced the Edict of Nantes, in which Henri IV had accorded liberty of religion to Protestants, aside Catholicism. This renunciation led to a massive move of Protestants (Huguenots) to Amsterdam and other places to the North, which enriched the culture and economy there, to the detriment of France.

Like many others, Maalouf narrates the conservative revolution that started, in the West, with Margaret Thatcher, followed by Ronald Reagan in the United States, in 1978–79. It was motivated by resistance and revulsion with respect to excesses of socialism, culminating in the miners' strike in England that caused a blackout, feelings that the indigent were being 'pampered' by social security, while being 'shy of work', and loss of traditional values of family and nation. The conservative revolution sought more 'evenness', in less government intervention, less social security, more market, in liberalisation and privatisation. 'Perfect competition', the professed ideal of capitalism, which sounds like equality, in fact led to an inexorable march towards inequality, dominance, concentration, in monopolies, oligopolies, and increasing inequality of income and wealth. As Maalouf shows, this occurs again and again in political history. Worldwide, the shift was furthered by the collapse of the Soviet Union and communism, which discredited the socialist drive towards egalitarianism.

The Soviet Union combined evenness of ownership, access and rights, formally at least, with evenness also in ideas, lack of variety and freedom of initiative and lack of opportunity for connecting ideas. That took out dynamism and innovativeness and broke up the union. The Iranian revolution, at the same time, was also anti-communist, but also anti-capitalist, and was conservative, in seeking a return to traditional religion, homogenising values and habits. This spread to other Muslim countries.

The best society lies in a combination of evenness, egalitarianism, in access, rights, legitimacy, with unevenness in ideas, allowing for diversity of views and initiative, and connectedness to allow cross-fertilisation of those ideas, enabling further cognitive and spiritual development. The first two have been characteristic of early liberalism, but with the conservative revolution the connectedness of people unravelled. Maalouf traced that to the revival of Adam Smith's *invisible hand*, which led to a surge of disconnection and egoism. This was not only a matter of greed for possessions, entertainment, enjoyment, power and attention, but also an urge of 'identity politics', in esconcing oneself in a fort of identity and from there combat others. It is also due to a lack of external threat that unifies. During the initial wave of the Corona virus, people came together, to some extent, in conformance to the shared regime of distancing, but when the virus receded, in some places, and then veered up again, people revert to their urge for individuality and diversion, and close contact, resisting the break-up of relations in social distancing, and they seem to retain that in the second wave of the virus. What to think of Dutch youngsters who seek diversion in the Belgian resort of Knokke, and create ruckus by violating the distancing imposed because of Corona, and engage in scuffles with the police, in protest against the closure of pubs at one o'clock at night?

Suppression by authorities of diverging ideas and their dissemination has gained enormous power with the use of new technologies of surveillance, for monitoring phones and hacking computers, desirable to fight terrorism and crime, but threatening privacy and opening up opportunities for control of thought and behaviour more widely. More heinous even is the disarming of diverging ideas by breaking down ideas in general, after the crumbling of truth, with fake news. In the absence of truth, control of expression is hardly needed. Unwelcome ideas can be disarmed by branding them as fake news.

Knowledge

An organism can only survive and stay alive when it is not a closed system, combating the process of increasing entropy by taking in energy in the form of food and excreting refuse. Increasing entropy has also been seen as loss of order, as when a body decays when no longer being fed. Order here is coherence of heterogeneous entities. When left alone in isolation, an organisation also dissipates, in a chaos, dissolution of order, with knowledge getting more even, losing specialties and novelty. A task of management is to prevent this, maintaining some variety and exchange with the environment.

A question I have in the theory of knowledge is this: Does new knowledge increase or decrease the entropy of a stock of knowledge? At first thought one may think that it increases entropy because it adds to the stock of possibilities. But this is not so if in fact the new knowledge invalidates much of existing knowledge, reducing the number of relevant elements, yielding integration and unification, reducing a number of laws to a few, which is what physics, for example, is continually trying to do, to increase order. The endeavour of the present book may also be seen in that way. In trying to find connections, similarities, in underlying fundamental principles of change, I try to reduce entropy. This does not apply to cultural products such as literature, music and pictorial art. We still marvel at old productions and treasure them.

In turning to a knowledge system, such as an organisation, let us distinguish the use of existing knowledge and the production of new knowledge. When the number of people in an organisation increases, the totality of knowledge produced and used by all people has decreasing returns to scale, as in the log function, due to information overload, gradually exhausting individual absorptive capacity, especially in present times, with a diversity of media, including social media, explosion of content, sources and channels, due to ease of access, n, so that the efficiency of information use increases less than proportionally to n, as according to the logarithm of n in entropy.

The production of new knowledge, on the other hand, arises from the interaction between people, so what counts is the number of connections between them. The number of possible direct connections between n components, is $n(n-1)/2$. On the one hand, this may clog up communication to the detriment of action and decision-making, but that may already be included in the increase of entropy. On the other hand, the number of possible connections increases the potential for novelty by interaction. The derivative, a measure of the increase of connections, is $n - 1/2$. Beyond the minimum of $n = 2$, the increase of potential combinations is greater than the increase of entropy, whose derivative is $1/n$. Thus, innovation potential increases faster than entropy, the loss of order. This formalises the claim that chaos gives opportunities. Perhaps this is a way to look at the difference between democracy and authoritarianism. In the latter, order is greater, but opportunities for renewal are smaller. The price for the higher order is more rigidity.

The model should be further refined. In other research, discussed above, I proposed 'optimal cognitive distance'. Higher cognitive distance increases misunderstanding, but at the same time increases the potential for innovative 'novel combinations'. The conclusion is that for innovation one should seek an 'optimal' distance – large enough to yield innovative potential, but no too large to realise it, due to lack of understanding. If understanding decreases linearly with distance d, and novelty potential increases linearly, productive outcome is a quadratic, inverse u–shaped function of distance. If understanding decreases linearly with distance, according to $1 - ad$, and novelty potential increases with bd, then optimum innovative performance I is achieved when $d = 1/2a$, and there $I = b/2a(1 - 1/2a)$.

If we take this into account, an increased number of potential combinations at too high a distance, in a fragmented society of people thinking differently too much to understand each other, innovative potential does not increase, and democracy will not realise its potential. Thus, like an organisation, a society should also have some focus of shared meanings and aims.

Organisational Focus

Here I continue the discussion of organisational focus, and the application of cognitive distance and entropy to organisations. This is less computational and perhaps easier to understand. Lachmann (1956) already, and later Tsoukas and

Chia (2002) took a process view of an organisation as a continual process of change, in interaction with its environment, as I proposed before as a general view of objects. Organisations are not to be seen as static objects that change, but, on the contrary, as constructs to stabilise change that occurs continually anyway, and may yield decay, in organisational structure and procedures. This stabilisation often overshoots into organisational inertia, and institutionalised myopia.

Organisational purpose is said to require 'organisational culture'. I found that a bit too vague, and proposed (Nooteboom 2009), that purpose is achieved by means of an organizational 'cognitive focus', which has both intellectual and moral/emotional features. The latter concerns how one arranges ways in which people deal with each other. A large organisation requires teams with some difference in focus, with teams that are to some extent autonomous, in a 'loosely coupled system' (Danneels 2003; Narayaman et al. 2011). Here, if we take focus as organisational identity, large organisations can have multiple identities (Kogut and Zander 1996). To function as a coordinated whole, organisations need some more or less specialised shared language or jargon, perceptions, set of ideas, understanding and morality, as part of organisational culture (Schein 1985). Without such focus, too much effort, time and aggravation would have to be spent to disambiguate meanings, eliminate misunderstanding, set priorities, establish directions, coordinate activities, align incentives and negotiate the terms of collaboration. Witt (2005) offered a related view of entrepreneurs and managers as providing 'cognitive leadership', which is largely to develop and maintain such focus. The focus of an organisation includes fundamental assumptions concerning the human being and its environment, concerning whether the human being is more self-centred or altruistic, risk is seen as a threat or opportunity, the world is to be mastered or submitted to, is predictable or uncertain, nature is to be exploited or saved.

A wider organisational focus has greater entropy. This is another puzzle: a wider focus entails more elements, and less concentration in a dominant perspective or practice, and hence larger entropy. On the other hand, there is more variety of perspective, which seems to indicate less evenness, and hence less entropy. Apparently we should distinguish between difference in 'content' and difference in 'weight', 'dominance', 'access'or 'legitimacy'. With wider focus, there is less dominance of one or a few perspectives. With more different perspectives of equal weight, or 'legitimacy', hence higher entropy, there are more possibilities of achieving 'novel combinations', and hence higher innovation potential. And when new knowledge is produced, in interaction, in 'novel combinations', entropy is reduced again, in invalidating old knowledge, in 'creative destruction'. In other words, the higher entropy of more elements can yield novel combinations that when successful reduce entropy, if those elements are connected.

In the system of many small, independent firms, in 'the industry' or 'the market', entropy is large. Within a firm, a production department is oriented at efficient production, and its focus is tight and entropy is small. To maintain consistency, only some views are legitimate. Within a large firm one can have a pocket of relatively wide focus, constituting 'corporate entrepreneurship', in a research or strategy department. It has a wide variety of different views, all legitimate, to breed novelty. In contrast with a small firm, it has the advantage of using the resources of the large firm, where risks are spread. But to still achieve some coherence between different departments, it is more constrained in its focus than an outside, independent entrepreneur. Production departments usually have tighter focus, to preserve systemic coherence for the sake of efficiency.

There is a stream in the literature of seeing entropy as overload of communication between units, crowding out work, increasing with the number of units n of an organisation (Janow 2003). I think this requires a different model than that of entropy. As discussed, with n units, the number of potential bilateral links between them is $n(n-1)/2$, which increases quadratically with n, thus more than proportionately with n, while $\log n$ increases less than proportionately. As the number of links increases, communication explodes and may crowd out work. That is why communication has been constrained by inserting hierarchical levels, restricting communication to the next higher and lower level, at the price of less contact between top and bottom of an organisation, and higher management becoming estranged from the work floor. An alternative is the 'hub and spoke' structure, with all communication going through the hub, apportioning only relevant information, not to unduly disturb work in the spokes. That has the drawback of delay and potential information overload in the hub.

If entropy is not this effect of the number of potential ties crowding out work, what is it due to? As discussed, it results from overload of an excess of information throughout the system, exceeding the absorptive capacity of its units, creating missed information, misunderstanding and diversion from work. Now, If we weigh the cognitive distances between any pair of links with the quadratic, inverse u–shaped utility function of distance, discussed before, we might obtain a measure of innovative potential.

How does focus work, and how is it implemented? On the competence side, focus is needed to *enable* people to understand each other and connect complementary knowledge, without unduly restricting variety and creativity. On the governance side, focus is needed to *motivate* people to collaborate and share and connect knowledge, without unduly restricting autonomy, ambition and competitive spirit. The larger the organisation, with multiple foci, the more the focus shifts away from the competence side to the governance side, to keep people 'on the same page'.

Organisational focus also has a function of both selection and adaptation of personnel. In selection, it serves to recruit people, often on the basis of self-selection of personnel joining the organisation because they feel affinity with it, and adaptation, in the socialisation and training of new personnel. To support these functions, focus must be embodied in some visible form. Such form is needed for several reasons. One is to function as a signalling device to outsiders. That is needed as a basis of the (self)selection process of incoming staff, and for recognition and identification by other stakeholders, such as customers and suppliers. For this, organisations develop their own specialised semiotic systems, in language, symbols, logos, role models, metaphors, myths and rituals, style of advertisement and external communication. This is what we call organisational culture. It differs between organisations to the extent that they have different goals and have accumulated different experiences, in different industries, technologies and markets. The central difference between firm and market is that in the former such focus is made and in the latter it is not, or to a much lesser extent. There still is a remaining, shared cognitive focus from shared national, regional or industrial culture, what Spender (1983) called 'industry recipes', and to some extent in collaborations with some shared understanding. Thus the market has the higher *potentiality* resulting from variety, and the firm has the higher *actuality* of performance.

Focus is a kind of myopia. The tighter it is, the greater the danger that it becomes a prison, locking in ideas and practices. To complement this myopia, one needs complementary ideas and practices from partners, at some cognitive distance. This makes that the notion of focus yields not only a theory of the firm but also a theory of inter-firm relations.

Mostly for the internal function of coordination, we find the exemplary behaviour of an organisational hero, often a founder of the organisation, corresponding myths and rituals. More formalised forms of organisation are procedures, for reporting, decision-making, recruitment, contracting and the like.

Science

Concerning the evolution of knowledge, particularly in science, the problems for evolutionary theory are even worse than discussed in the previous chapter. The issue of interactors and replicators was discussed there. It is not entirely clear what the success criterion of selection is for knowledge. In biology it was survival. What does that mean in science? Do knowledge workers die when their ideas fail? It is their ideas that die, in the sense of not receiving attention and recognition. When ideas are selected out, eliminated, this decreases entropy; replication initially increases entropy but enables novel combinations that may again reduce entropy.

Kuhn (1970) famously claimed that scientists do not seek falsification of theory, as Popper (1959) said they should. That is too much to expect. Their scientific achievements form the basis for reputation and rewards in the form of further careers and room for further research, and they often seek to protect those by trying to confirm rather than falsify their theories. Falsification is more a matter of competition between scientists in the 'forum' of a scientific community, mostly via journals. Popper later granted that it is rational to hold on to theories and milk them for all they are worth and to find out where their real limitations lie (Lakatos and Musgrave 1970).

In evolutionary terms, communities of scientists in 'research programmes' would be 'species', and, as argued before, for evolutionary theory to work, there must be 'isolating mechanisms' between them to prevent species from mixing. In industries there is some evidence of such isolation, with distinctive industry structures and logics ('recipes'). But it is a known source of innovation when boundaries between industries are crossed, in 'novel combinations', as professed by Joseph Schumpeter. A prime example is the Internet, as a combination of the formerly separate industries of computing and communication.

Here also, replication in communication, publications, meetings at conferences and seminars and PhD training, is more a matter of reduction of cognitive complication, generalisation and reconstruction in more sparse terms than a matter of replication. As in the case of organisations and their capabilities, in science, the survival and replication of purported replicators is not entirely dependent on success of interactors under selection. Unsuccessful results may also be replicated. Here, in some disciplines more than in others, (even) more opportunities exist to mould the selection environment than in the case of firms in markets, in opportunities to create a selection environment of dedicated scientific associations with their proprietary journals.

Scholarly societies, or disciplines, schools of thought, or research programmes, may perhaps be seen as species. What, then, would be the 'isolating mechanisms' here? Like organisations in general, scientific societies have a shared cognitive focus of basic assumptions and views, in a 'hard core' of assumptions and method (Lakatos 1978). Different research programmes do seem to have such mechanisms, in 'protective belts', and this generates misunderstanding and disagreement concerning what is relevant in debates between such programmes. That is an effective isolating mechanism. Scientific journals are often attached to such schools, and are not open to submissions from rival schools. Rejected or ignored groups then often institute their own proprietary journals. In this way, there are obstacles to interdisciplinarity. From an evolutionary perspective that is a good thing, in the separation of species. But this is perhaps one of the reasons to add to the doubt of the validity of evolutionary theory concerning science. There is symbiosis between species, but in science it is rare. Scientists want to tend to their familiar turf. Yet, we applaud interdisciplinarity, for its novel combinations in innovation, and some of it happens.

A case that I know of is 'behavioural economics', which, contrary to previous assumptions in economics of full rationality, employs insights concerning unreflected, subconscious choice, on the basis of non-rational behavioural heuristics. However, I have heard from applied psychologists that they turn away from collaborating on this with economists, because there also economists want to force everything into the framework of rational optimising choice, while the point is that this is not and cannot be done. I will come back to that later, in Chapter 4.

Change of Knowledge

How does knowledge develop? One 'logic of change' is found in evolutionary theory, as discussed. Another form was already argued by Aristotle. In 'entelechy', change of form arises from the realisation of potential. An example is the oak that grows from the acorn. We now have the knowledge of DNA that generates bodily forms. Hegel proposed that we get to know something in its limits and failures. We can perhaps see in what way failure can unmask those limits. The question next is to what extent and how the realisation of potential can in its limits generate the emergence of new potential, in what the philosopher Schelling called 'potentialisation'.

For change of knowledge, in the evolutionary literature, some authors have allowed for variations that are guided from a higher level, variety-generating 'search' routines (Nelson and Winter 1982). In the literature of the school of Austrian economics, Kirzner (1973) proposed that entrepreneurs are 'alert' to opportunities for renewal. The business strategy literature suggests that there are higher-level *dynamic capabilities* that direct the change of lower-level capabilities (Teece et al. 1997). Teece (2007) characterised dynamic capabilities as 'not allocating means to ends, (but) discover and create new ends and means'. Dynamic capabilities are said to entail 'scanning, sense-making and decision-making'. Narayaman et al. (2011) proposed that they include rational inference of cause-and-effect relations, rules for experimentation and ability to utilise organisational memory. They also include exchange of codified knowledge with others. These proposals are largely tautological, or empty, labels on our ignorance. What do 'alertness' and 'scanning' mean? Dynamic capability is 'capability at discovery of new ends and means'. How does all that work?

Zollo and Winter (2002) discussed 'deliberate' as opposed to 'experiential' learning. Is deliberate learning separate from experience? So, the question now is to what extent, and how, organisations can develop dynamic capabilities to escape from inertia. How is it a process? Opportunities that an entrepreneur 'finds', in 'scanning', is discussed as if they are already lying somewhere, ready to be discovered. In what sense, and to what extent is this search blind? How is it related to evolutionary selection, and to what extent can it anticipate survival in selection? Teece (2007) does recognise that opportunities are not found but made. How is that done? On page 1323, he states,'One must accumulate and then filter information from professional and social contacts to create a conjecture or a hypothesis about the likely evolution of technologies, customer needs, and marketplace responses.' I find that too vague. I think such processes need to be accompanied by experimentation, interaction with the environment of markets and institutions. Teece and others do recognise that customers and suppliers can offer ideas for innovation, in 'open innovation' (Chesbrough 2003). However, they seem to assume that there is first the 'sensing' and subsequently the 'seizing' of an opportunity, again as if it already subsists. I propose that the sensing and shaping of an opportunity occurs in trying things out and seizing them for further development if they are fruitful. There is talk of 'adapting' to the 'ecosystem' of markets, institutions and firms. But the ecosystem is also a process, being affected by innovation.

To respond to these issues, I use my 'cycle of discovery', inspired by the work of Jean Piaget, developed in earlier work (Nooteboom 2000). That claims to apply to individual people as well as organisations. It has largely been ignored by the literature of dynamic capabilities.

According to this work, cognition develops from *assimilating* experience into existing ideas ('frames') and *accommodating* them, developing new frames, when this fails.[1] This opens up the black box of 'scanning' opportunities. It can be both deliberate and accidental. It shows a process of how learning arises from experimentation, in interaction with the environment.

---

[1] See Flavell (1967), 'The developmental psychology of Jean Piaget'. The work of Piaget goes back to the 1930s–1950s, and has met with considerable criticism, which led to replication and extension of his experiments in different ways, some of which confirmed his claims while others contradicted them. Thus his thought became controversial, but overall it still stands and remains included in modern textbooks of developmental psychology (Leman et al. 2019). The crux here, in the present book, is the notion that cognition develops from action, in assimilation and accommodation, which does not seem to be contested.

The basic idea is that new ideas arise by applying an old idea in new settings, where it is confronted with new challenges to survival, with conditions in which it does not fully fit. Here we again have an increase of entropy to open up to the production of new order, which subsequently reduces entropy again. For that, established practice is *generalised*, that is, brought into new environments where it meets new challenges of survival. To survive, the product or idea has to adapt. This can take the form of retrying options that formerly failed. This requires organisational memory, in documents or in the experience of older staff. This leaves the basic structure, or *architecture* (Henderson and Clark 1990), the same, by varying the choice of elements in the architecture of existing repertoires, in *differentiation*, allowing different options. When that is not adequate, the next step is to incorporate, into the existing architecture, elements from a local idea that is successful where one's own is not. This will take the form of adopting elements from successful local practices, perhaps adopting entire local practices, fitted into existing overall structure, called *reciprocation*. This yields hybrids of old and new elements. This is akin to the logic of metaphor: one learns to see something familiar in in the light of something different and new.

This amalgamation of old and new elements, pressed into an old 'basic design' or logic yields hybrids, a familiar phenomenon in the history of innovation (Mokyr 1990),. The stage of *hybridization* is important for exploring the potential of foreign elements without yet making the sacrifice of dumping existing basic logic or design. This stage also allows one to explore where the problems lie, in the integration of old and new, and what, in the existing structure, limits the full utilisation of new potential, and this gives hints into what direction promising more structural change might lie.

This may lead to the next stage, where one makes experiments with more structural change, in '*accommodation*', in different configurations or ' architectures' of old and reconfigured or new elements, to reinstitute order, but a new order, in a new structure. Here an attempt is made at reduction of entropy, by eliminating redundancy and overlap. When a new basic design emerges, initially it is far from perfect, may not yet realise its full potential, and may for a long time carry along residuals from the old logic that hamper efficiency and full breakthrough of the novelty, in '*consolidation*'.

On paintings by Turner, one sees the parallel existence of new, somewhat lumbering steam boats and elegant old sailing ships. In the transition from building wooden bridges to that of iron bridges, at first the old constructive principle of 'swallow tails' to connect wooden parts was maintained, while with iron there is the alternative of welding. In an analysis of artillery practice it was found that at the firing of the cannon, one soldier backed up a few steps, more than needed to protect himself from the recoil of the gun. Why?

The conclusion was that this was a leftover from old-time horse-drawn artillery, where at firing someone had to step back to hold the horses in their fright at the explosion.

The breakthrough of a novel design, and its subsequent improvement and refinement, is gradual but fast relative to the long process of transferring the old product or idea to a new field, making minor adjustments, creating hybrids and tinkering with attempts at structural change.

The cycle of discovery shows how transformation is not ongoing flux, but requires the alternation of stability and change, increasing and decreasing entropy, in assimilation and accommodation. One needs time to discover where the limits of validity of the old lie, and to experiment with variations and shifts. In this, there is much trial and error, but also inference of possibilities for adaptation.

The process is recognisable in the literature on innovation of firms by internationalisation. While formerly internationalisation was primarily a strategy to maintain growth after saturation of home markets, it unintendedly set in motion the process of discovery, which companies then started to identify and understand as such, and subsequently started to employ as a deliberate strategy of innovation. This mode of operation was confirmed in a conversation with a former CEO of Shell: They did originally engage in internationalisation only to increase sales, until they found out that this yields innovation, after which they adopted it as a deliberate strategy. This illustrates how the process can yield a change of organisational focus, from an orientation at expansion of the market and economy of scale to allowing for divergence for learning.

The 'logic' explains also why innovation by collaboration, at appropriate cognitive distance, between individuals, is effective. Having to explain one's knowledge and practice to a partner entails a step of generalisation, where one obtains new insights into the limits of one's views and practice, yielding a need to adjust, first on the basis of reframing it based on previous experience. Next, when that does not work, partners in collaboration offer each other sources of reciprocation, in an exchange of novel elements to try out, and in exchanging design principles in search of solving the constraints and problems that arise from the resulting hybrids. It is much easier to have a partner with a different but experienced view to stimulate and assist the process than having to do everything by one's own inference.

This may contribute to a deeper understanding of the familiar notion of 'absorptive capacity': having more experience, one is better able to reframe, in cognition and competence, what a partner offers in the process of reciprocation. Earlier, I indicated that the other side of the coin of learning by interaction is rhetorical ability, to help a partner absorb what one offers to him, notably by the use of apt metaphors. The more experience one has, the greater the fund of one's metaphors is.

March (1991) distinguished between exploitation, the use and incremental improvement of resources, and exploration, the more radical, architectural change of basic design or logic. The challenge is to combine the two. The cycle of discovery alternates them: differentiation and reciprocation are incremental, exploitative, but prepare for the exploration of accommodation, and consolidation is exploitation again.

One can see similarity of the cycle to the Yin and Yang cycle of Taoism. Both are an unending circular alternation of complementary principles of change and adaptation. If one wants, one can see assimilation as Yin, yielding, and accommodating, and creating the new as Yang. I am not sure that would yield any additional insight, but it is intriguing.

Coming back to evolutionary theory, there is literature on *punctuated equilibria* in technological development (Gersick 1991; Romanelli and Tushman 1994; Tushman and Anderson 1986; Tushman and Romanelli 1985). While detecting that phenomenon empirically, this literature has not offered an adequate theoretical explanation. As noted in Nooteboom (2000), in evolutionary biology Eldredge and Gould (1972) offered at least the beginning of an explanation of punctuated equilibria, on the basis of 'allopatric speciation'. There, the origin of new species is attributed to a long process outside of, or at the margin of, parent niches, where there are challenges and opportunities for experimentation with novel forms without their being swamped by the dominant species in the parent niche. Punctuation is rare, relative to long periods of stability, because it takes a long process of outside trial and error to establish a new form that is strong enough to turn around and successfully invade the parent niche. This point of evolutionary 'logic' resembles the principle of generalisation in the 'cycle of discovery' set out here, with its exit to a novel context of application. However, upon scrutiny, the underlying logic is different. In evolutionary theory it is only the criteria of selection that change, offering new challenges and opportunities for survival and reproduction that cause a phylogenetic drift away from the parent population since interbreeding is blocked by some physical obstacle to interaction. Here, by contrast, the novel environment is a source of novel insights into limitations of existing practice, a build-up of motivation to change, and, most importantly, suggestions for novel elements that might be tried out, in hybridisation, and novel architectural principles to eliminate problems caused by hybrids. Also, while the shift of environment may be imposed unexpectedly from the outside, when disaster strikes or an invading competence destroying innovation or disaster forces one to adapt, it may also be undertaken voluntarily and by design, in a deliberate step into a novel context of application, seeking optimal cognitive distance.

A key question in the discussion of evolutionary theory was how blind this source of 'variation' is. It is blind in the sense that the innovative outcome of the process cannot be predicted. However, it is not blind in that novel selection environments can be selected purposely, as likely to generate opportunities to continue exploitation while yielding novel challenges and indications of elements and directions for exploration. The process is informed by past success and failure in selection. Applying Campbell's (1974) criteria of blindness, variations from the process are not independent, are not separate from the environment, and later variations can be corrections of former ones. They are correlated with the solution, in the sense that experience with failure and indications of solutions inform the process. However, the outcome still cannot be predicted.

A question is again whether new knowledge increases or decreases entropy. It will reduce entropy when the variety of possibilities decreases, in making part of prior knowledge invalid and redundant, or creating unification, in a reduced number of natural laws or other explanatory principles. What happens to entropy along the cycle of discovery? In generalisation of an explanatory framework or technology to a new field or market, the number of applications, the number of alternative configurations, increases and entropy increases. In the next step of reciprocation, hybrids are made of the familiar and the new, in new combinations. There, perhaps, one can say that entropy begins to decrease, in attempts at the unification of old and new. Then, one finds inconsistencies or inefficiencies in the novel combinations: it is seen where the old hampers the use of the new, in inconsistencies, obstacles, inefficiencies in duplications or detours, which gives an incentive and insights in possible 'cleaning up', in leaving out redundancies and detours, in accommodation. That can be seen as reducing entropy. When the emerging novelty is further streamlined, entropy further decreases, but then it diverges in different applications of the new, fitting different environments, and entropy increases again. Thus, the development of novelty is not a uniform process of either increase or decrease of entropy, but an alternation of the two.

I propose that this is a more general principle: forms of life are a process of development with an alternation of increase and decrease of entropy, in breaking down structures and then building up new ones. In economic systems, globalisation leads to a unification and homogenisation of products and cultures over the world, an increase of entropy, and it reduces the sources of variation that yield novelty, so that in this unification development may stagnate. However, there is an increasing diversity of forms of democracy and autocracy, and corresponding institutions.

From the cycle of discovery one can deduce several forms of entrepreneurship or dynamic capabilities. There is the stage of taking a practice into a new environment, in 'generalisation', with a widening of focus, not yet on the competence side, but on the governance side, of opening up to new institutions and environmental culture. In the stage of differentiation one relaxes focus to allow for the renewed try-out of old practices, and in the stage of reciprocation the opening up is more on the competence side, of trying out elements from outside, local practices, in hybridisation. This requires a departure from the strategy of merely enlarging turnover, holding on to the standardisation needed for economy of scale. In accommodation, the departure from the old focus is more radical, allowing for structural change in basic architecture. Consolidation is again more incremental, and the focus narrows again, directed at increase of efficiency, and then there is differentiation of the product to optimise market fit.

If everything changes, can change change? The principle that to change something, a theory, a practice, a product, one way is to carry it into new environments in the form of new areas of application or markets, as developed above, seems pretty stable, but other logics of change may exist or emerge.

Uncertainty

The difference between risk and uncertainty is that in the first, probabilities can be attached to possibilities, and one can engage in probabilistic calculation, while in the latter not all possibilities can be identified, so that probabilities cannot be attached (Knight 1921). With environmental uncertainty, one can still conduct scenario analysis, imagining some possible futures and investigating the robustness of options under the difference between those futures, that is, yielding reasonable though possibly not optimal outcomes in those different futures, favouring robustness over optimum. If one has knowledge of the way in which things work, by what logic, but not its outcomes, as in evolution, one can conduct a computer simulation to explore outcomes, notably in 'agent-based simulation', where every different agent is simulated in interaction with others.

Uncertainty can refer to outside states of nature or society: in 'environmental uncertainty', one's inner capability to assess or calculate, the extent and truth of one's knowledge, options for action, preferences, outcomes of actions, their value, or 'behavioural uncertainty', in the conduct of partners or rivals.

The human being will never have full certainty concerning all of these. According to Johannes Climacus, one of the pseudonyms of the philosopher Kierkegaard, we suffer from a 'common shipwreck' of uncertainty, and in his '*Johannes Climacus, or De omnibus dubitandum est*', methodic doubt, of everything, is a characteristic of philosophy. According to Kierkegaard this leads to desperation, and rescue from it requires faith, for him faith in God. Elsewhere, Kierkegaard pleads for action, and choices by the individual, along its path of life, in an uncertain world, and for that one needs trust or confidence, and for that again God is needed. I think we can do without God, but one needs a basis, with hope and taken-for-granted points of departure, assumptions as a basis for giving direction in the movement along that path.

In other words, ideology or taken-for-granted and often tacit background assumptions are unavoidable. It is 'focus' on the larger scale of a society, beyond organisations, and a barrier to the increase of entropy with ideas flying off in all directions. However, such ideologies or background assumptions create prejudice, and to escape from it, the only thing one can do is to subject it to discussion, in recognition that one is not certain. For that, organisations need outside partners. Countries need internal variety and international relations. My motto is 'imperfection on the move'. Nothing we do is perfect, which does not mean that we should be content with whatever we know, and it is subject to improvement, though the result will also be imperfect. To break an opening to a change of view one needs opposition from the other, with a different point of view.

As indicated earlier, assimilation of knowledge is to a greater or lesser extent accompanied by expansion or unification of knowledge, and it can lead to a break and transformation of the interpretative structures that constitute absorptive capacity. In that sense, communication not only yields 'replication', but also contributes to the generation of variety. In communication, expression by the 'sender', tacit knowledge can never be fully codified and externalised so that expressed knowledge is always incomplete, and in absorption, or assimilation, knowledge is complemented and supplemented from the existing cognitive framework of the 'recipient'. Furthermore, what is 'left out' by the sender and what is 'added' by the receiver, and how this is done, depends on clues from the context. Thus, meaning is always context dependent (though not completely context determined).

In firms, knowledge that is tacit or locked up in a 'community of practice' is more resistant than codified knowledge to 'spillover' to competitors and thereby loss of competitive advantage, but when knowledge is tacit, locked up, in part, in individuals, the firm is vulnerable to loss of knowledge due to personnel turnover.

How blind is variation by collaboration? Collaboration requires communication and as indicated this is always imperfect, and can yield unintended and unnoticed variation. That is one reason why collaboration is blind in the sense that it is subject to more or less random disturbance and fluctuation of interpretation and meaning. It is also blind in the sense that one cannot predict the precise outcome of learning by interaction. However, it is not blind in that it is informed by selective success: one selects partners in learning who have demonstrated to be competent, at sufficient but not too large cognitive distance, and contexts that allow for interaction. There is some design: one may have a fair guess of cognitive distance and select partners at close to optimal distance. Applying Campbell's (1974) criteria of blindness, variations from collaboration are not independent, and later variations can be corrections of former ones. They are not, however, correlated with the solution in the strong sense that the outcome can be predicted.

Truth

A distinction has been made in philosophy between analytic truth that are truths by definition or following from axioms, as in mathematics, and synthetic truth about facts in the world. I do not believe in the latter in terms of objective or final truth, and go along with the Kantian thesis that we do not know things as they are 'in themselves'. In fact, I believe we don't know whether, in what sense and in what way we know things in themselves, but we know them through mental frames of perception and interpretation, in the form of neuronal networks in the brain, and it is prudent to doubt their perfection, completeness and fixity. Kant's view that time is a continuous flow and space is fixed and uniform is now being replaced, in modern physics, with the idea that they are quantified, 'granular' and connected in space-time.

A dire effect of the lack of objective facts, even in science, is that people have started taking facts as mere 'opinions' or 'views', messing up news and discrediting science, and claiming that everyone has a 'right to his own truth', or 'alternative facts'. This undermines not only science but also democracy.

From the pragmatic philosopher John Dewey I adopt the notion of 'warranted assertion', according to which an assertion is to be supported by 'warrants' of facts where they can still be found, as is often the case, and logic, 'plausibility', defined as coherence with other accepted 'truths', and the success of a theory in its 'working', that is, its practical consequences, in answering to the goals engaged in. It is in contrast with the lack of respect for facts, logic and practical workability of conspiracy theories that are in ascendance. Above all, it seeks falsification, in contrast with the attention only to confirmation of conspiracy theory.

We can think without language, but language gives great leverage to thought. Language is a means of conceptualisation. In several ways, I will try to show the development of meaning, the process of language, is similar to evolution and the cycle of discovery discussed in the present chapter. That is the subject of the following chapter. There, I will again focus on process: How do meanings arise, of words and sentences, what happens in their use, and how do they change?

Chapter 3

LANGUAGE

Wittgenstein said that there can be no private language. If on a deserted island I bump my toe on a stone and call the darned thing 'clink', and the next time I call it 'clunk', there is no one to correct me. My reference to things with a word can fly off in all directions. If I think something I cannot 'unthink' it. It is, Wittgenstein said, like having pain: it is odd to say that you 'think' you have a pain.

I accept from G. H. Mead (2011) that language started out with bodily gestures and expressions and vocal gestures such as cries and shouts. Gestures and language are needed to learn from interaction with people, in communication, sharing and opposing meanings of words and gestures. As Mead argued, we develop a sense of self and consciousness by expressing ourselves, observing reactions of others, reacting to those and observing our reaction. Perhaps that is why young people flock together and find it difficult to observe the corona rule against proximity. On the other hand, distance contact by telephone rather than bodily proximity has also increased distance. Gestures and facial expressions are still important in communication, so that during the lockdown due to corona, communication in writing only did not suffice and we had to bring in visual contact, via applications like Zoom. But to many that is a poor substitute for physical proximity and bodily contact.

The old idea of meaning was that it is reference. With the word 'chair' we refer to an object of that nature, or all objects of that kind. This leads to the issue of knowledge and truth as correspondence of ideas with items in reality. As discussed before, Kant raised fundamental doubt on this. From the Kantian view, it is very dubious to claim that words, linguistic expressions, actually do refer in that sense.

Reference, I proposed earlier, is intentional, not ontological: people intend to refer to reality, leaving aside whether, or in what sense, and to what extent, they actually do. However, words are not always only intended to refer. 'Speech acts' are performative, for example, to express emotion, utter oaths, get people to do something, or not to do it. Advertising, in business and politics, is propositional, in part, informing us of properties of a product, but it is mostly 'illocutionary', appealing to ancient tribal emotions that make you feel you 'belong' to a brand. In the *New York Review of Books*, Joseph O'Neill (28 May 2020) proposed that in US politics Republicans are much better at it than Democrats. To preserve the brand, Republicans unite even behind Trump.

Sense and Reference

Several philosophers deny the notion of 'reference', which suggests that something is 'present' and its name is somehow a label on it. Underlying it is the correspondence theory of truth and meaning. I deny this ontological claim. However, let us look at how words are used, as Wittgenstein recommended. From a pragmatic perspective words are used to do things with. Much of that is intentional. In this doing, collaboration is elementary, even foundational, as argued earlier and elaborated in this chapter. There, in collaboration, we need to talk *about* things. This 'aboutness' is *intended* reference, apart from whether, or in what sense they actually correspond with things. A word is needed to recognise a thing and to talk about it.

Next to 'reference', 'what is given', or what an expression is about, Gottlob Frege added 'sense' as a second dimension of meaning: of how some given object manifests itself ('die Art des Gegebenseins': the way in which things are given) (Thiel 1965).

In analytic philosophy, there has been a debate on sameness of meaning, using the principle (attributed to Leibniz), that two expressions have the same meaning if they can substitute for each other in a proposition 'salva veritate', preserving the truth of the proposition. Famously, this does not work in 'intentional and modal contexts' (discussed, notably, by Quine). An example of an intentional context is belief: 'Jack believes that Aristotle was a teacher of Alexander the Great.' This cannot be substituted by 'Jack believes that a pupil of Plato's was a teacher of Alexander the Great', even though in fact Aristotle was that, because Jack may not know this. There is sameness of reference but not sameness of sense. An example of a 'modal' context is necessity. The number of seas (seven) is equal to the number of capital sins, but that is not necessarily so. So, sameness of reference is no guarantee for sameness of meaning in all contexts. A solution was proposed in 'possible world semantics': two expressions have the same meaning if they have the same reference in all possible worlds. But identification across possible worlds is problematic, and it turns out to require a return to essence as what connects an identity across worlds, in 'trans-world heir lines' (Hintikka 1929), which is problematic for those who want to get away from essences, like me.

Sense can raise ambiguity, as a form of uncertainty, concerning reference, since that depends on sense as how one establishes reference. People can identify things differently. Symbols and arts also have meaning, in the sense that they affect sense, the way we look at things or listen to them.

Attempts were made to preserve the reduction of meaning to the logically clear and determinate notion of reference, to avoid the more fuzzy, subjective, psychological notion of meaning as sense, as how an object is identified as something. Here, in this book, the intention, by contrast, is to preserve sense, not only because logic requires it, but because it is a source of variety and change of meaning, playing a central role in the process of language.

Here, I shift the meaning of sense from the objective, Fregean meaning of 'how an object manifests itself' to the subjective 'how people do the identification', 'how they see something as …'. It is a property not of the object but of the subject. This is not ontological but cognitive. The classic example is that of Venus, which can be seen as 'the evening star' and as 'the morning star'. People observe Venus as the one or the other. Sense develops from 'associations' that people have built up along the course of their lives, which they use as what I will call 'identifiers': whether they saw the 'star' in the morning or in the evening. Experience can shift how things are identified, and 'as what' they are identified, in sense, and then also shifting reference. In Fregean semantics, the reference of a proposition was its truth value. Sense, then, is how one establishes truth. Here, I shift the notion of truth to the notion of warranted assertion offered in pragmatism, as discussed in Chapter 2.

Sense is personal, developed from experience along one's path of life. One may, for example, have a connotation of 'chair' from a memory of granddad's chair, reclining, with curved armrests of polished mahogany, and upholstery of blue-grey velours, fastened with buttons. When sense between people is widely shared, it becomes public, as a basis for communication. So, with a twist, I maintain Frege's distinction between sense and reference.

Further inspiration can be found in de Saussure's distinction between 'parole', the idiosyncratic, diachronic spoken word, and 'langue', the synchronic, intersubjective order of meaning. I will elaborate on that below. Concerning this order, as Wittgenstein said, 'There is no private language.'

What is the relation between word and sentence? Frege proposed that the meaning of a sentence is a function, in the mathematical sense, here by logic, grammar and syntax, of the meanings of words in the sentence, in 'upward causation'. But the reverse applies as well: the meaning of a word depends on the sentence it is in, and the context of action in which the sentence appears, in 'downward causation'. When one hears 'He sat on his chair at the desk' that pretty much, but not totally, settles what kind of chair it is. As Wittgenstein (1976) said, if you want to know what the meaning of a word is, see how it is used.

Language supports reasoned reflection, but how far can that go? It requires consciousness, and in dreams it goes astray. How conscious can a person be? We could not be conscious of all that occurs in our bodies and our actions. Our limited capacity for reasoned reflection could not handle that. Cognition and feeling are embodied and interwoven in unreflected bodily processes of metabolism. This entails a denial of the idea of a Cartesian separation between body and mind. Much in the body is determined by the unconscious operation of a variety of hormones, sugars, oxygen, red and white blood cells, viruses, bacteria, antibodies – which function in the operation of muscles and neurons, produce bodily reflexes in the so-called autonomous nerve system and cognitive reflexes and impulses in parts of the brain, in visual, auditory and proprioceptive perception. Thankfully, imagine that it all were conscious. Then we could not cope with it. But if much of human being is subconscious, how, in what sense can the individual have an identity? Isn't consciousness 'needed to keep things together'? To function coherently and survive, the body must have some coherence. That is not to say it is known how that unity of the self works on the level of neurons. In some way the human being creates a virtual world of its environment and itself in it. That is partly conscious, but largely unconscious. We experience the result but not its construction. Metzinger (2009) called this 'transparence': we 'see' through it. The eye does not see itself. Coherence also lies in the life narrative in which one is the lead actor, more or less goal-oriented.

Consider the issue of free will. Many choices are made subconsciously on the basis of 'tacit' routines. Bergson (1969) characterised consciousness as making choices, on the basis of memory and perception, in anticipation of the future. I think that choices can be subconscious, routinised. Of some choices one becomes aware after they are made, and one often gives an attractive twist to it, with rationalisations after the fact that did not in fact determine the choice. But in many choices the conscious does contribute in advance to the choice, in supplying the 'input' and 'trigger' of subconscious decision-making. The conscious also often participates in the execution of subconscious choices.

How about punishment for bad conduct? Does that make sense if the underlying decision is subconscious, so that 'one could not help doing it'? It remains sensible as 'input' to the development of unconscious decision processes, which incorporate experienced success. In sum, the proposition is that while conscious processes are not 'in control', they do have influence. In the conscious execution of subconscious choice one can still exert some influence and direction to one's life.

Sentences settle word meaning in two ways. They settle the intended reference, of a propositional sentence, picking out specific senses of words in the sentence from their multitudes of sense, which help to establish the 'truth' or impact of the sentence. In terms of entropy, sense harbours a multitude of possible meanings that collapses into a determinate reference.

Langue and Parole

The notion of 'parole', adopted from Saussure, is a feature of individual, idiosyncratic, context-dependent usage, is 'progressive', that is, can yield new personal sense, with only a small chance that it will be adopted in public sense, langue, which is conservative, to provide the stability and mutual understanding that communication requires.

Some time ago, in a newspaper there was a picture of a man sitting on a cow, in his living room. It was a stuffed cow, with a dent on its back for the seat. The caption of the picture said: 'See him sitting in his cow.' This is an idiosyncratic addition to the sense of a cow. After this, when one passes a field of cows one may wonder how it would be to have one of them as a seat, but this sense is not likely to become part of the public, shared sense of a cow.

Poetry gives a prime illustration of how sense works. In using words with a surprising reference, out of context or in a surprising context, it shifts repertoires of sense or adds to them. This is a salient case of how art affects sense. Previously distinct words, without overlap of their repertoires of sense, are connected, in a surprising fashion, creating an overlap of sense, in the new context of the poem, not only by surprising reference, but also by an unusual connection of meanings by sound, in assonance and alliteration (Fry 2005). The positioning and connection of words that generate such 'associations' are sometimes generated by the needs of rhythm or the formality of the poem (it is a Shakespearian sonnet, say). That has been said to yield an argument against 'free verse' that lacks the 'benign terror' of connection by rhyme or metre imposed by form. The formal form forces one not to be satisfied with the most immediate choice of a word, and to look further afield for a more surprising connection.

The twist or extension of sense, triggered by the poem, often is only local, in the poem, in an 'event on the page, instead of referring to something off the page' (Dobyns 2011), so that it hardly contributes to the public order of langue. Some senses do spill over in langue, such as calling a beloved a 'rose'.

A related phenomenon is metaphor, where something (the 'target') is posed in terms of something else (the 'source'). This again transfers sense from one word to the other. This can be very useful in 'crossing cognitive distance', by seeing something unfamiliar in the light of something familiar, to trigger understanding. In this way, something like poetry can aid innovation.

What is the difference between speech and writing? Speech has a personal listener, directly or through a bilateral communication channel, in interaction, or one-directional, as by radio or TV, and writing has a reader, one-directional, anonymous and at a different time. Speech has sound, writing does not. The written remains, the said does not. Speech is primary, in the sense that in evolution it was first, children speak before they write, and some speakers never learn to write. As investigated by Derrida, writing is 'derived' from speaking, a representation of it. In its joint temporality, speech reflects the process nature of language more. Writing suggests that with its permanence meaning is stagnant – 'is' and stays, is 'present', with a fixed identity, like an object.

Saussure focused on the order and structure of langue rather than the anarchic parole. I am more interested in parole, as a form of change. There is, I think, a connection of parole with Derrida's notion of 'deconstruction'. There, one tries to escape from the existing order of a concept or theory. But every outbreak is followed by a new imprisonment. Every new foundation, everything specific, is a new limitation. We cannot say everything at the same time, so what we say or think is inevitably partial and biased, and what we repeat is not the same, has an aura of differentiation, according to the context. Hence Derrida's 'deconstruction' is automatic, inevitable, not conscious destruction. One is perhaps tempted to see deconstruction as negative, purely destructive, nihilistic, but it is (re)constructive.

We can try to analyse things, including expressions, in breaking them up into their constituents, but the pretention often is that this yields a 'rock bottom', fixed and indubitable, context-independent fundament, whereas in fact it is fluid, amenable to shift and re-interpretation, depending on the context and the change of knowledge and meaning. Here I recall Wittgenstein's notion of 'meaning as use' (Wittgenstein 1976). Since use is open-ended, with new uses emerging, meanings change. I recall that not only do the parts determine the whole, but also, vice versa, the whole affects the parts, the meaning of a word depending on the sentence it is in, and the meaning of the sentence changing according to its use, in different action contexts.

How, then, does meaning change? The sense of a thing, as a repertoire of features associated with it from memory, is not to be seen as a repository of fixed things waiting to be selected for establishing reference. They are not only triggered by the context at hand but are also already affected by it. Memory is not retrieval but reconstruction on occasion of experience in a new context. So sense is a potential, with new realisations depending on context. Parole is the motor of this.

Here, one may use the notion of a 'script' (Abelson 1976; Shank and Abelson 1977). A script is a structure, a composition, of connected nodes. It can be a model of a practice, a process, logic, theory and sentences. It has an 'upward causation' of how the nodes constitute the script, and 'downward causation' of how the script enables and constrains the nodes. The word 'logos', translated as 'logic', or 'rationality', originally derives from a notion of composition, bringing together (Oger 1995, 63), from the Latin 'legein', which means reading out, naming, collecting (Dutch *Van Dale Etymological Dictionary*). The script is a model of that. This again is connected with pragmatism, logic as how something 'fits together' and 'works'. It is also a convenient tool in the 'praxeology' of economics, advocated by Lachmann (1978). It is also useful in innovation theory: if an innovation does not fit in the script of the user, its adoption is difficult, necessitating a change of the user script.

The script notion applies generally, for example, as the 'primary' process of production in an organisation. To connect with an earlier discussion, it is a model of a complex adaptive system (CAS), as moving, having a degree of entropy, in the number and difference of roles of nodes, whose action is constrained in its place in the script. The entropy of a script with n units of equal incidence is $\log n$.

A script is intended as constant, like a method, to be applied again and again. But it is always incomplete, with tacit underlying assumptions that are taken for granted. In the restaurant script, for example, it is not specified that one is to put the food into one's mouth, not into one's pocket. However, some restaurants do allow for 'doggy bags' to take remains of food home. Paying by check was a node but is now rarely used, replaced by cards. Each node has its own range of admissible subscripts, such as paying cash or submitting a pin code of a card.

New processes may sprout from the nodes, as from the nodes of a rhizome, which I mentioned before, in the introduction, when discussing Deleuze. The connections between nodes can denote temporal, causal or logical sequence. In an organisation it is a model of a causal and temporal sequence of production, where one part of the whole project produces and passes a component of a product on to another part, for integrating it in a connected structure. In language it is the logical, grammatical and syntactic coherence of words. The link between nodes can also indicate a shared use of some resource, or a common method.

The classical case is that of a restaurant (Shank and Abelson 1977), with nodes of arrival, entry, seating, choice of food, serving, eating, payment, departure. In a self-service restaurant, the order of nodes changes: arrival, food selection, payment, seating, eating and departure. This does not leave the nodes unchanged. Seating now includes carrying a tray of food to a table. Different activities can be 'substituted' in a node, such as the different forms in the payment node: cash, credit card, debit card, smart phone. The nodes are not necessarily the same in every restaurant; there may be chopsticks instead of cutlery, for example. There are also superscripts, such as the location of the restaurant, with its insertion into systems of services, provision of utilities, logistics and parking around the restaurant.

Professional practice entails using a script, but also supplementing or adjusting it, in 'tinkering' with it. Levy Strauss called it 'bricolage' ('do it yourself'). You have to learn it, or grow into it. The practice is often learned in something like a master–apprentice relation. Not everything in the practice can be specified and codified in a manual. The practice is too rich for that, that is, has so many incompletely specifiable elements that can change from one context to another. The adjustment is not random experimentation, but directed to the purpose. This is discussed in the literature on 'communities of practice' (Brown and Duguid 1996). A novice has to participate in 'peripheral participation' before he/she is a seasoned practitioner. That flies in the face of a tendency to try and specify the practice completely, in a protocol, as happened in a system change for the operation of markets in healthcare in hospitals. Fixed protocols of legitimate practice were needed for insurance companies to conduct evaluation for the approval of funding. This was born from the old notion of practice as something fixed and present that could be seen as rigorous, complete and constant. But an organisation chart rarely represents actual lines of communication and collaboration, and the improvisations needed for actual practice. Such formal structures arise from a fear of chaos, lack of confidence in flexibility, lack of trust, and the desire for reliability and control to avoid risks, which is never completely possible.

Take the sentence as a script, and the word as a node, with connections between the nodes according to logic, grammar and syntax. In downward causation, the sentence (script) limits what potential meanings of the word (node) are 'admissible', can 'work'. But that does not necessarily leave such admissible sense unaffected. The sentence and its action context may clarify or 'tweak' it. The story about someone sitting at a desk may show that the chair has no backrest. That is unusual, but it can make sense and may then be added to the repertoire of the sense of 'deskchair'. I told how once I saw a picture in a newspaper of someone siting on a stuffed cow. Even the stuffed cow may henceforth be part of the connotation, the sense, of 'chair'.

Would it help to apply the 'cycle of discovery', in the change of knowledge, discussed in the Chapter 2? That would mean that a fundamental change of sense could arise in shifting the word to a new context, finding that it fails there, in inadequate reference, try to adapt it by introducing sense from other words that work in the new context, experimenting with hybrids, in preparation of a more fundamental, 'structural' change. What would that mean here?

Hermeneutic Circle

A model of meaning change has been offered in the form of the 'hermeneutic circle'. For the hermeneutic circle, George Gadamer (1975) employed the notion of the 'syntagmatic' and the 'paradigmatic' axis. In the hermeneutic circle, concepts from the paradigmatic axis are selected to come together in a sentence, on the syntagmatic axis, and there clouds of sense collapse into specific references. There is a connection here with the classic difference between Plato's view of particulars (here meanings in sentences) as being reflections of fixed universal concepts, which constitute 'real reality'. However, general concepts may change from their use in specific sentences and settings. Parole can shift langue. Then, surprising combinations from sense in the sentence may alter clouds of sense on the paradigmatic axis.

The question still remains when and how an identity breaking change of sense occurs. Perhaps, as in the logic of the cycle of discovery, this happens when in a new context a word adopts a sense that does not cohere well in the cloud and then a new concept arises, perhaps with the same word, with a change of the repertoire of sense of the concept allowing it to fit in sentences where it could not have made sense before. A new content of a node (word meaning) may open up new scripts (sentences) in which it fits. The stuffed cow as a chair, if adopted widely, may then allow the word 'chair' to appear in a new script of producing chairs from stuffed cows, in a spin-off from the ordinary butchery business, and a new branch in the furniture business.

The understanding of an abstract or new concept is best triggered by an example, an illustration, in aiding sense, moving from the syntagmatic to the paradigmatic axis.

How about differences between languages? Are different words for more or less the same concept different manifestations of the same meaning, or do they have different linguistic identities? No doubt, most such words, say 'chair' and the French 'chaise', have an overlap of sense. However, for some concepts there are two words in one language and only one in another. In English there is 'faith' and 'belief', while in Dutch there is only one word. For some words it is difficult to find a proper translation, such as the German Hegelian term of 'Aufhebung': eliminating the old sense of a concept by lifting it up to a higher level. In different languages, sentences obtain their coherence, structure, from different grammars and syntax. I therefore think that across languages words should be seen as different objects.

As discussed, poetry can shift sense, by means of metaphor, where an object is seen in terms of another type of object, and in metonymy, where it is seen in terms of a similar object, or rhyme or juxtaposition in rhythm.

Fishing for compliments is a metaphor, fishing for pearls is a metonymy, since fishing for fish and for pearls share a similar relation to the sea, and compliments don't.

General, public concepts, 'universals', can be taken not as essences but as *prototypes*. Prototypes are characteristic examples representing the general. But in individual usage, as discussed, new senses arise from language use, with a shift or tweak of the universal, to such an extent that its essence seems dubious. Should the notion of essence be dropped, perhaps? Would prototype serve to replace it? Here, as in the case of the notion of reference, the notion of sense may be cognitive and intentional rather than ontological.

Here again, in the hermeneutic circle, we find an alternation of an increase and decrease of entropy, as in the cycle of discovery in learning. In the application of a word in a sentence, selected from the syntagmatic axis, entropy is reduced, in eliminating most potential meanings, but in the process its meaning may shift, adding to the repertoire of possible references of a word, in an increase of entropy.

Complementarity?

Here, I try out a line of thought inspired by quantum physics, not as a direct causal connection with it, but as the inspiration of a possible model in language, with the 'Copenhagen interpretation' of 'complementarity'. Is there some kind of complementarity between reference and sense? According to the Copenhagen interpretation, an elementary particle is both a particle and a wave, a 'cloud' of probabilities of location, and when the particle is observed, the wave 'collapses' to a determinate position, with the probability of one location becoming 100 per cent and probabilities of all other locations becoming 0 per cent.

There is no universal agreement on this. How can a particle be both a particle and a wave? Some say that the quantum calculations are confirmed and that the wave is not intended as a reality, prior to observation. In positivist science one looks only at what is observed, and to speak about what happens outside observation is meaningless. That is not tenable, as discussed earlier. Some, like Einstein, held that a physical theory should be about reality and should explain it, also when not observed. The theory of complementarity seems to imply a conflict with Einstein's relativity theory, which implies that the velocity of light is a maximum velocity, while the Copenhagen interpretation implies *non-locality*, that is, immediate action between some particles at any distance. I will not go into that debate, and will not take a position in it.

The question here is whether there is any meaningful sense of complementarity in language between reference and sense. Could it be that sense is a 'cloud' of sense, potential identifiers, in the sense of features by which one identifies an object as this particular chair or any other chair, and arguments by which one considers a proposition 'true' or 'warranted', when confronted with other words, in a sentence, 'bumping into' them, so to speak, or a sentence 'bumping into' an action context, and the 'cloud' of possible identifiers 'collapses' into a single actuality, a reference? For example, a chair may have five, four, three or no legs (a box to sit on), with or without the rollers of a desk chair, all colours, a variety of material (wood, cloth, metal) and so on. A specific chair referred to has determinate, fixed properties, but that becomes clear only in the bundling of words in a sentence.

The use of sense would be a subjective assessment, in the process of finding reference, and the context and responses of others may invalidate it. It is 'parole'. If it 'works', in the sense that it is not invalidated, and yields a shared reference between people, it can be adopted as a shared intersubjective or public reference, in 'langue'.

To connect this with the hermeneutic circle: the 'clouds' of sense are on the paradigmatic axis, and the collapse to reference, in langue, occurs on the syntagmatic axis of the sentence. Anomalies lead to adjustments to the clouds of sense of the words involved; identifiers may drop out or additions may be made.

Cognitive distance between people then is the extent that clouds of sense overlap, with shared identifiers. It determines the extent to which the people involved identify things or warrants of assertions in the same way.

Object Bias

I propose, as a further conjecture, that we have a disposition, inscribed by evolution, to look at reality in metaphor from material objects in time and space (as proposed by Gary Lakoff and Mark Johnson 1980), rather than as the process of sense-making that it is. For example, we conceive of light as the property of an object, while it is wavelength of light as a process, reflected from an object.

I propose that this bias can be understood as arising from evolution, as claimed by evolutionary psychology. This way of looking at the world in terms of things was needed for survival of the human being and its evolution, or so I propose. It goes back to the 400,000 years of humans as hunter-gatherers, when for survival it was crucial to adequately perceive the speed and direction of the sabre-toothed tiger, enemies, prey, the trajectory of a spear, the location of a lost child. It was adaptive to identify and recognise material objects and people, and their movement. Action was action mostly on physical objects, things or people, and as a basis for that it is not functional to see them as processes. Change that was relevant was movement in space of an entity considered fixed.

This idea was proposed before by Henri Bergson (1969). In evolution, in the need to act for survival, there must be stability of things to identify and recognise them (family, child, food, foe) and act upon them. This is not unreasonable, founded on the condition that their change is slow relative to the action context. A stone is change, in terms of moving elementary particles, but this is irrelevant when throwing the stone. Bergson proposed that we misconceive time by spatialising it: we conceive time as a succession of states like separate things juxtaposed in space. We conceive of intensity as size: extension in space. Rather, an increase of pain is, he claims, an extension of things involved in it: cells, nerves, body fluids. He pleads for a notion of 'duration', as continuity, where what happened before is integrated in what happens now, in a unity, like hearing a melody from notes strung together.

The problem now is that abstract things, such as identity, justice, happiness, meaning and trust, are not like material objects and do not behave like objects in time and space. Sense here is not adequate to its task of identification. If you carry a chair from one room to another, it remains the same, but if you carry the word 'chair' from one sentence to another, its meaning will change, as if a chair drops a leg or changes colour. Present survival of humanity may require a shift of metaphor to adequately deal with the abstractions that now dominate life and public debate. In the current development of humanity, it is crucial to see that things change: people, opinions, habits, meanings. What they mean depends on the context. Perhaps the puzzling results of modern physics may give a new metaphor for meaning.

It is also understandable that in the urge to act, attention goes to the short term, where the change is smaller than in the long term, while currently there is a need to look at the long term, to grasp the deterioration of the environment, the long-term development of man and of robots, and exigencies as that of the corona virus that has now engulfed humanity, with the attendant need to protect against similar viruses to come.

In particular, an important part of the object bias is the *container metaphor*: we are 'in' love, 'in' a mess, 'in' a bad state and so on. This plagues the discussion of identity, and the metaphor is so basic, so much a foundation of thought and language, that one is not even aware of using a metaphor. There is a need to become aware of this.

Admittedly all this is just conjecture. In a discussion of morality and ethics, in Chapter 5, I will also give the evolutionary argument that in a long history of the human being in hunter-gatherer societies the need to collaborate, in defence and hunting, yielded an adaptive advantage in developing empathy, imagining the position of the person one collaborated with, and later a more generalised sense of symbiosis. Here, the idea of someone as a thing moving in time and space is expanded with a notion of the other person having intentions and feelings. I conjecture that this was fitted into the object bias as 'direction', going somewhere, and led to the idea of someone wanting something or in moving away in fear. Another manifestation of the object bias is that virtues are seen as properties we have or not, as things rather than the practices they are, in life as a process, as something we are, rather than as a thing we have. In this way, a whole constellation of thought and language could have been built up from the basic bias, creating a misunderstood world that now turns against us.

How about humour? Humour arises from incongruity, discrepancies: an action, idea or word does not fit the context, or violates common usage or logic. The low can be presented as the high, the high as the low. For example, 'You are too excellent for someone of your high rank.' Laughter and smiling can complement, ingratiate, endear, express love or gratitude and encourage. It can ridicule, relieve tension, puncture power, break down utopia or relativise. It can accompany sceptical pragmatism or irony. It can soothe disappointment, soften despair, make uncertainty less threatening, show up absurdity and make it amusing, disarm nihilism (Marmysz 2003), serve reconciliation, and can be pre-emptive: laughing before you are laughed at. It can be condescending, even threatening. It can yield distraction, evasion, avoidance of challenge, risk and ambition. It can show embarrassment. It can break up order, as a Nietzschean, Dionysian force. It can be a dung beetle to decrepit, moribund illusions. It is so multifarious that it requires some system.

According to Henri Bergson (1969), on the one hand, life should aim at a balance between memory, with its ideas, routines, habits, established meanings that constitute ability, with its purported truths, ideology, things taken for granted, prejudices, rigidity, inflexibility and myopia and, on the other hand, adaptation to what is perceived in the here and now. Humour is often a disturbance of this balance. An illustration Bergson gives is that of a short man bending over as he passes through a high doorway. Imbalance on either side, in maintaining an old practice or idea in new context, or randomly jumping into new ones can be a source of humour: in mindless, unreflective, neurotic impulse, on the side of adaptation, and rigidity or obstinacy, on the side of memory. Sticking to something that does not work. Holding a match to an electric light. Shaking a locked door, opening an umbrella in the sun, using a screwdriver as a hammer. Bergson characterises it as turning man into a mechanism, presenting it as a thing, a puppet on a string, without will or consciousness.

Humour can be a metaphor misfired: 'He looked like a million dollars: all crumpled and green.' Or reversion: someone falling into the trap he set for another, such as a robber robbed. It can desacralise the sacred, as a king on slippers. It also includes vanity, as preoccupation with what one developed as an individual, in the past, and neglect of what one now bumps into, failing to recognise others, like a pompous professor. Bergson noted that there can be humour in two series of events interfering with each other, such as when a fight story interferes with a love story, or when an embrace becomes a wrestle, or when a laboratory story interfering with a circus story, with a scientist dropping a glass vial being presented as missing a grasp in the trapeze.

Language is the process in which people interact. That interaction, of the individual in society, is the core theme of the present book. It is discussed in the next chapter.

Chapter 4

INDIVIDUAL AND SOCIETY

Identity

This chapter is the central one in this book. Previous chapters were preparatory. The theme of individual and society, or self and other, is an old one in philosophy, sociology, political science, anthropology and economics. I will make use of those disciplines when relevant.

There is confusion concerning the notion of identity. First, a distinction needs to be made between personal and collective, cultural identity. The two are connected. People can hardly develop in isolation, so that personal identity needs cultural identity to feed upon, and, vice versa, people contribute to cultural identity. So, identity is inherently relational.

I will first turn to personal identity. David Hume said that there is no coherent, identifiable identity, but only an incoherent buzz of impressions and feelings. That cannot be true. First, he himself granted that impressions yield more or less stable and coherent ideas that are more or less consistent with each other. Further, if they were not coherent, the body would be unable to survive. Body and mind are intertwined, with neuronal circuits guiding interdependent bodily processes, partly unconsciously, and formed in that process, in adaptation to survival and flourishing.

Fukuyama (2018) claimed that identity arises from *thymos*, interpreted as the urge to distinguish oneself, to gain reputation. That is certainly part of thymos, but identity cannot be reduced to it. One cannot reduce all initiative, such as that of a discoverer, entrepreneur, scientist or artist, to egotistic or narcissistic desire. I hold that the good life is a combination of pleasure and sense, in contributing to something beyond yourself, which can be done in many ways, and if for that one develops and exploits one's talents, it is pleasurable. That can be a means to a goal of riches or reputation but can also have intrinsic value, in the challenge and excitement, the ethics and the thymos that the building and using of talents involves.

In his early philosophy, Jean Jacques Rousseau celebrated the freedom of the individual to act according to its nature, freed from the suffocation and mental mutilation of the individual by the collective. Later he switched to the opposite, where shared public interest and opinion force the individual to conform unconditionally to the 'general will' (*volonté générale*), as opposed to partial, parochial interests of subgroups. This led the French Revolution astray in its 'virtuous terror' and suspicion of all leaders as representing special interests. If your individual will did not correspond with the general will, that was your fault, and you had to admit that your view is wrong. That has been a source of inspiration for authoritarian regimes. If, under the Soviet regime, you did not admit you were wrong, you belonged in an asylum. A similar switch of view as that of Rousseau occurred to Heidegger, who at first exhorted people not to conform to the mass ('das Man'), and to go one's own way, he later conformed to the totalitarian Nazi regime.

Identity is an intriguing term, suggesting one is identical to oneself, remaining the same. A ubiquitous view is that character is fixed. Richard Rorty defined the self as 'an internally coherent set of beliefs and desires'. What does 'coherent' mean here? It seems to allow for different parts of the self. The whole of the self is wobbly, fragmented, opaque and changeable, within the constraints of inherited talents and environment. Yet it has a certain unity and stability, in its own body.

Authenticity

The foregoing suggests that identity can be multiple, perhaps even in conflict with itself, and susceptible to shifts, where mental construction and destruction continue. This is in line with the 'neural darwinism' of Edelman, discussed in Chapter 2. If the self is in ongoing development, then if 'authenticity', is being 'true to yourself', what does that mean? How can one be true to something that is still in development and one does not fully know? The idea of a self that is given and fixed and manifests itself in life without change is not only unrealistic but also repulsive, as if you are locked in prison, forever condemned to an original self. Is authenticity perhaps development, in the potential for it, in interaction with the environment and especially other persons that affect the realisation of that potential?

For the development of the self one needs both kinds of freedom: negative freedom in the paucity of external constraints and positive freedom in access to the necessary resources. There is much talk of authenticity, and it is confusing. Sometimes it is about the nationalistic idea that one is a 'real' American, Englishman or European. At other times it means the apparent opposite: that one distinguishes oneself from others, as a unique person. This reflects the difference between cultural and individual identity. To prevent confusion, I propose to reserve the term 'authenticity' for the individual kind.

However, the issue is not that simple. Personal identity builds from interaction with others and that requires some kind of community. Complete authenticity is impossible, since it would require isolation, enclosing one in solipsism, robbing oneself of the sources of identity. Cultures vary between those more oriented to individual identity and those more oriented to the collective. As I noted before, and implied in Heidegger's notion of existence ('Dasein'), and suggested earlier by Kierkegaard, and alive in pragmatism, the construction of the self takes place by acting in the world, so that one cannot be fully authentic in the sense of being autonomous, as economists do assume. I recall the earlier discussion of complex adaptive systems: subsystems (here people) connect to produce a higher-level system and gain new functions (positive freedom) but inevitably pay the price of less room for independent action (negative freedom).

Another problem for authenticity is that much of our choice is made subconsciously, spontaneously, triggered by circumstance: a gesture, something said, advertising, an event. How can you can be subconsciously authentic? This subconscious influence has already for a long time been exploited in advertising, and this has exploded in the use by 'platform companies' that mine data concerning our choices for processing in algorithms in order to individually target messages of advertising or political influence. This is accompanied by convenient free services of search and dissemination that are appreciated and used in spite of violation of privacy. Though I cannot assess all the legal ins and outs, it seems that there must be ways to maintain private ownership of the data at their source, the individual, and to tax their use for commercial purposes. However, it is predictable that then the free services offered to harvest data will be reduced or will carry a price.

Humour can help to hide, confuse, circumvent or ridicule established order, or to confirm, soften or hide it. Bergson indicated that the difference between the art of a tragedy and the amusement of a comedy is that the first aims at the individual, closer to authenticity, at odds with conformity, while a comedy aims at stereotypes, adhering to conformance to the point of absurdity.

Violating norms of conformity can derail into immorality, and be met with indignation and anger. Less extremely, the deviation can be not immoral but unsocial, as exhibited in current deviance from corona measures.

As discussed earlier, in linguistics, Ferdinand de Saussure (1979) distinguished between langue' and 'parole'. Parole yields negative freedom, some absence of constraint, individual usage of words, with a meaning that changes in time ('diachronically'), with idiosyncratic connotations that are not the same between people, and only overlap in partially shared reference. It may block positive freedom, in lack of access to resources, due to misunderstanding or isolation.

Parole and sense make language vague, up to a point, with room for variation of meaning around what is customary. Ambiguity is usually condemned, but it can be a good thing, because it gives some room to hide in the penumbra of meaning it creates, at the edge of common meaning, and to meddle with one's own deviation, attaching some respectability to one's idiosyncrasy. Poets can get away with violating logic, linguistic rules or habits.

Causality of Action

For the analysis of interaction between people, we need a causality of action. This is found in the multiple causality of Aristotle, as follows:

Type of cause

– Efficient:
  Agents or forces that do things: individuals, organisations, government agencies, unions, elites, political groups, racial groups, classes, employers, management, workers, immigrants.
– Final:
  Why agents do things: goals, aims of projects, views on the good life, values, ethics, power, wealth, art, recreation, sport, exercise, adventure, excitement, travel, economic growth, knowledge, science, preservation of nature.
– Material:
  With what are things done: loans, wealth, natural resources, infrastructure (roads, telecommunication, airports), housing, information.
– Formal:
  How are things done: mechanisms, knowledge, skills, technology, education, habits, myths, rituals.
– Conditional:
  What circumstances affect action: Markets, institutions, laws, trust, freedoms, climate, safety, viruses, geography, fashion, festivities, religion, networks, urbanisation.
– Exemplary:
  What examples are followed: images, role models, designs, graphs.

In his criticism of Bergsonian duration, Gaston Bachelard (1950) took causation as a paradigmatic example of discontinuity, in the separation of cause and effect. But here one cause can be simultaneous with another, in the continuity of action; the final, material, formal and conditional causes persist during action, though they may change in the course of it, among others, by feedback of action upon those conditions.

The conditional cause can be of different kinds. It can enable or constrain. It affects the other causes. It can affect the final cause: labour regulations, corruption, social contacts. It can take the form of removing an obstacle. Take a waterway with a sluice. The water presses on the sluice door, and opening that door releases the water. This is like Bergson's 'triggering' of a process. The freezing of a canal provides the ground for skating, where to enable gliding the pressure of the narrow iron of the skate melts the ice. On the sea between Sweden and Finland it can be so cold that there is car racing on the ice: the weight of the car is not enough to melt the ice and make the car slide.

Aristotle made the mistake of assigning a final cause to nature, which was dealt a death blow by Francis Bacon. Since then, causality developed into a mechanical process, such as colliding billiard balls, and then causality became a purely formal consistent succession of cause and effect. In the eighteenth century, David Hume showed that regular succession does not prove a law, since there is no logical necessity of the uniformity of nature, with ongoing succession of the presumed cause and effect. To accept a regularity as law-like, one needs to adduce a causal process that is plausible in the sense of aligning with what is accepted in the results of science (Nooteboom 1992).

An irony of the history of ideas is that economists strive for mechanical causality in equilibria of supply and demand, while Aristotelian multiple causality, including the final cause, is eminently fit to deal with human action in the economy, with markets and institutions as conditional causes. Institutions as rules of the game are clearly part of the conditional cause. So is the exemplary cause, giving an example to be followed, in mimicry. The final cause is clearly not a rule, though it may be a habit, but more a spontaneous drive, akin to a virtue. The material causes may be self-made or adopted from the environment. The formal cause may be like a rule or habit, imposed by training or a profession or may be self-constructed, spontaneous or tacit. Multiple causality may be used to distinguish virtues from institutions or to distinguish between different institutions.

Elites

One is regularly subjected to an 'Elite', and populism exploits that, in playing the underdog, while aspiring to pursue an elite position itself, hypocritically, in the endeavour to submit the people to the leader. 'Elite' is a spooky concept. It appeals to the imagination, and to a sense of envy, resentment and victimisation, and a penchant for conspiracy theory. It is also justified to some extent, in many people being neglected, misunderstood or patronised, exacerbated by their being more highly educated than formerly, which is felt to justify a greater influence on public policy. But what, exactly, does 'elite' mean? It takes different forms.

One sense is that of exceptional performance, as in the army (elite troops), in sports (stars) or among scientists (wizards). And, why not, top chefs, bakers or plumbers. Such elites of performance serve as role models, or as compensation for one's own felt mediocrity in providing glitter by proxy.

In another sense, elites are composed of people with an unusual ability or possibly undeserved position to govern. This can concern political, legal and scientific professionals. They exert power and often form an 'in-crowd', sharing power and enhancing it in concert. This is often dressed up with an ideology, which is more or less arbitrary and parochial, but is presented as self-evident and objectively necessary. It is used by some to maintain their position, and to distinguish themselves from 'the suckers who did not get it'. Pierre Bourdieu called that 'symbolic violence'. There lies a source of populism, where the leader opposes an elite and then builds it up for himself.

The present protest against incumbent political leadership often is that in fact they do not have the competence they claim, and do not take the responsibility for leading and serving the people, but serve their self-interest. The prestige of scientific leaders, professors, has been eroded by scandals of meddling with data, analysis and conclusions in research. Judicial powers have lost prestige, through a suspicion of incompetence, class justice, lack of openness and the use of obfuscating language. Leaders of firms are accused of obsession with profits and remuneration, at the expense of workers and the environment, with pressure on governments with the threat to withdraw the employment they offer unless they get advantages in lenient regulation, low taxes and subsidies. Postmodern thought avers that truth does not exist, and everyone has a right to his truth. So, how can authorities of all kinds claim a superior truth? Who do they think they are?

But the shoe pinches also on the other foot, the citizen itself. It is easy to blame the elites, but how valid is that? Under the libertarian ideology of markets, with an urge towards privatisation and market dynamics, also in public services, citizens were told they are customers, and in markets they have learned that 'the customer is king' and 'is always right'. So now they treat public servants as they are accustomed to treat hairdressers and pizza bakers. Doctors have to supply the treatment and pills that the Internet says are best, and teachers must supply the degrees pupils have a right to.

Wary of electoral loss, politicians draw in their horns to the demands of vociferous citizens and do not fulfil their responsibility for being honest concerning what is needed for society, for example, in environmental policy. Do not touch car usage, distant holiday flights and meat consumption. Some leaders howl along with the wolves, against European integration, immigration and Islam.

Societies need elites because not everyone has the talent and ability, dedication and resilience needed for public service. However, to avoid entrenchment of an elite in its bulwark, appointments to their positions should be open to outsiders. The carousel of jobs for insiders should stop. On the other hand, citizens should recognise that they are not consumers but participants in 'civil society', and share responsibility for it.

Cultural Identity

Now how about collective, cultural identity? 'Culture' has several meanings. First, as opposed to nature, as man-made. Second, in the anthropological sense, ways of life of a group, with its habits, rules, norms, and underlying ideas of the human being and society. A third meaning of culture is the legacy of cultural products of art, architecture, literature, science, law, theatre and so on. This last is also called 'civilisation'.

The multiple causality of Aristotle can help here:

> Concerning conditions, in culture there are, for instance, Hofstede's 'power distance', uncertainty avoidance, masculinity/femininity (achievement/harmony), and individualism/collectivism.

Causality often goes both ways, in feedback. Culture results from many variables, but also affects them: the variables interact. Lack of law may create aggression. Many causes come from the past. A people's distant past of herding may have engendered aggression because in the footlooseness of herding the control by law was scarce, and the resulting culture of aggression and revenge may have persisted even when there was no more herding.

Clearly, culture is associated with the notions of social system and society. Those can be wider, as in a nation, or narrower, as in a region, municipality or organisation. One can hardly ascribe a group average to an individual. Insofar as a feature is behavioural, within the group it can vary much or little between individuals, depending on how homogeneous the culture is. Different relations may carry different values: one may be oriented at equality and benevolence at home, and at authority and rivalry at work. Some concepts have different meanings in different cultures. Friendship may be seen as contribution to the meaning of life, in challenges, or shared pleasures or interests, or may be seen as more in terms of support and forbearance.

Are there any true universals of conduct, applying equally everywhere? It has widely been found, in different cultures, that there is a 'consistent tendency to socialise girls more towards nurturance, responsibility and obedience; boys towards independence, self-reliance and achievement' (Smith and Bond 1993, 71–72). Also, 'a substantial world-wide consensus [was found] about different gender roles. Men were believed to be higher on dominance, autonomy, aggression, exhibition, achievement and endurance. Women were believed to be higher on abasement, affiliation, deference, succourance and nurturance.' These differences were found to be less in more developed and rich countries than in poor ones. There were also cross-country similarities in mate preference and in differences in that between men and women. 'Men tended to evaluate potential mates more on the basis of youth, health and beauty, while women tended to pay more attention to earning capacity, fidelity, ambition and industriousness.' There are evolutionary arguments for this: beauty is associated with fertility in women, and ambition and industriousness as a source of earning and protection in man. Women, one story goes, are attracted towards infidelity with strong and beautiful men, while partnering with a faithful one. But men and women were found to have similar attention to mutual attraction, dependable character, emotional stability and maturity, and on qualities of being understanding, intelligent, exciting and healthy. One study found that the second most highly desired attribute of a mate was dependable character, but another study found large differences in attitudes to marital infidelity. Apparently, infidelity is thought to be a sign of undependability in some countries but not in others. When one looks at behaviour in more detail, as in what behaviours indicate infidelity, there are great differences between cultures. In some it is hugging, in others flirting and in others dancing with someone else than the partner. Differences between people will increase when one looks at behaviour in more detail (Smith and Bond 1993), not only what people think and do, but how, precisely, they do it.

Fairly general also was the decoding of emotions from facial expressions. However, when one allowed subjects to identify and categorise emotions themselves, rather than presenting them with pre-conceived ones, differences showed up, and only some emotions were shown to be recognised generally. Cultural difference, such as whether it is individualistically or collectively oriented, affects how the expression of emotions is valued, and differences in that between different types of emotions.

Many studies have been conducted on the basis of the 'World Value Survey' (WVS) that has now been running for 30 years. In one of those, on the basis of the 'sixth wave 'of the WVS (2010–14), with 258 questions and 85,000 respondents in 60 countries, Inglehart and Welzel (2014) constructed a map in which those countries could be located. This was constructed from 10 traits constructed from 8 questions: on happiness, trust, respect for authority, voice, importance of God, tolerance of homosexuality and abortion, national pride, post-materialism, social values and obedience/independence. From the traits were constructed two 'principal components' that formed the axes of the space on the map. The first axis ran from 'survival values' (importance of God, low trust, low voice) to 'self-expression values' (tolerance, independence, low nationalism, low authority, respect), the second axis from 'low level of happiness and materialism' to 'high level of happiness and post-materialism'. The two axes yielded four quadrants: (1) with 'survival values and materialism', with, for example, India, Romania, Mexico, Armenia, Jordan, Algeria; (2) labelled 'self-expression-materialist', with, for example, Russia, China and 'Confucian' countries; (3) labelled 'survival-post-materialist, with a number of African/Islamic and some South Asian and Latin-American countries; (4) labelled 'self- expression and post-materialist', with, for example, Sweden, Germany, the Netherlands and the Uzrom – this one can construct a measure of distance between countries, taking into account connections between features.

In sum: 'There *are* gender differences that transcend cultures. We *can* all decode certain facial expressions. Personality traits *do* cluster in similar ways, Humans *are* all capable of both aggression and social behaviour. Dimensions of organisational structure *are* relatively invariant' (Smith and Bond 1993, 93). Many overall features show a difference between individualistic and collectivist cultures. An example is that motives or reasons for conduct in individualistic countries are attributed more to personal features and in collectivist countries more to circumstances.

Do cultures change, and is there convergence of culture between nations? For a while, convergence seemed to take place, in a march, considered inexorable, towards neoliberalism and globalisation, supremacy of markets, which has been shown to go together with increased individualism and the erosion of communitarian values. But a trend towards 'modernism' can go together with new combinations of old cultural values in some areas, as in market dynamism combined with authoritarian rule. Elsewhere, one can now see the beginnings of a turnaround, with increasing resistance to unfettered markets and more attention to communitarian values.

There is a resurgence of authoritarian regimes and of nationalism, in the EU there is deviance from some liberal democratic values in some Central European countries. Culture is affected by external conditions of climate, with more frequent tornados, and desiccation, the spread of the coronavirus and a migration crisis. Corona is impeding globalisation, and has affected views regarding privacy and limitations of freedoms of association and movement.

Culture is a complex adaptive system (CAS), with many interacting variables in feedback loops that yield unpredictable outcomes (Holland 1992).

Technology and culture mutually affect each other. The Internet has enormously increased opportunities for production and dissemination of ideas, apps, films, photos, with online media, and corresponding entrepreneurship. It has also produced new opportunities for surveillance, affecting privacy, effected in some countries more than in others. Nations can be progressive or conservative in producing and adopting technology.

Does every arbitrary group, such as an organisation, have a culture? It certainly has it in the anthropological sense: it exhibits a distinctive array of rules, habits, routines, myths, rituals and ideas of the organisation's 'mission' and basic ideas about whether man is primarily self-regarding or altruistic, master of its destiny or subject to fate or environmental imposition such as the coronavirus, rational or emotional, rule-following or anarchistic. In an earlier analysis, in Chapter 1, I proposed the idea of an 'organisational focus'.

An organisation may have culture also in the form of material legacy: its possessions, legacies and art. Those yield mutually enforcing means for collective identity, supporting the focus of the organisation. Organisations will reflect values from national cultures, more or less, but where this is the case, they still vary in the ways in which they enact those values in practices. For example, an individualist national culture may be organised hierarchically and formally, which may be authoritarian or not, with personal accountability or group responsibility, or it may be organised more informally and bottom-up. This depends on the industry and on whether the organisation has a focus on efficient exploitation or novelty in exploration.

Discussion about European identity concerns collective, cultural identity – in common laws and regulations – permeability of borders, exchange and trade, and shared civilisation and some underlying philosophy. It is important, however, to keep in mind concerning both organisations and associations such as the EU that behind collective identity there remains personal identity, with individuals developing along a unique path of life. The notion of collective identity labours under a misconception, due, I conjecture, to the 'object bias', discussed before. Intuitively, in the 'container metaphor', identity tends to be seen in terms of a box one is in or out, and you cannot be in two boxes at the same time. So you have either a national or a European identity, cannot have both, you have to choose. And if you are not in the same box as I, we have nothing in common. Race also is seen as a sharply delineated box, where you are in or out. The box suggests homogeneity within it. But if identity is being in some conceptual box, with others with the same identity, where does that leave personal identity?

Networks

An alternative way of looking at identity is in terms not of containers but of networks, with an individual seen as a node in various networks. As a person, one can be positioned in different, partly overlapping networks at the same time, connecting people in ties that are direct or indirect, via an intermediary agent. Ties bear different forms of capital: economic, social, cognitive, political and symbolic (as proposed by Pierre Bourdieu). Symbolic capital includes norms and ethics of conduct, and their expression in symbols and rituals. Personal identity builds on the networks one is in, and thus one has a wider scope and reach of identity to the extent that one is involved in more networks. Identity shrinks when the subject is left outside the networks. The ties are cemented by mutual dependence, their cultural and symbolic capital such as shared myths, canonical stories and histories, role models, proverbs, sayings, which, here again, can be national but also, in different networks, related to family, job, profession, community and so on.

In networks of people, the individuals need to have sufficient width and depth of knowledge to yield the 'absorptive capacity' of dealing with other people at some 'cognitive distance'. It follows that the less education and experience one has, the more difficult it is to profit from networks.

From this perspective, in terms of networks, collective identity is seen as a relatively dense set of connected networks, with many and relatively strong connections or 'ties'. 'Strong' here means frequent interactions, 'multiplexity', that is, a variety of contents (economic, social, cognitive, cultural, symbolic) per tie, continuity (not ad hoc but lasting) and investments dedicated to the tie (economic, emotional). Particularly strong ties arise among family, friends, colleagues, sports clubs, religious denominations, ideologies and so on. National identity is weaker, unless it is connected with ideology, particularly when that is related to race, religion, strengthened by symbols of some heroic past. Apart from that, in what way is national identity stronger than European identity?

Pierre Bourdieu (2018) distinguished two types of societal structure: a social one, which arises in less developed countries, and a capitalist structure in developed countries. In the first, social positions of authority, prestige, leadership, delegation and public service are not institutionalised but have to be earned and constantly maintained with gifts, attention, favours, or intimidation and violence. Crucially, it is not so much a matter of quid pro quo between individuals, as in capitalism, but of social acceptance and sanction. Sometimes these relations are romanticised, but underneath the apparently humane reciprocation of gifts and values of community there are more or less hypocritically hidden economic interests and dependencies. The power may appear soft, but it is there.

In developed capitalist societies, by contrast, social position is documented and established once and for all, by legal ownership, legally or politically backed appointments, educational and professional diplomas and membership of associations. It all began with writing, settling issues without the ambiguities, impermanence and forgetfulness of the spoken word. The development made for a great increase of efficiency, in not having to continually maintain, service the position, and achieving clarity and stability of position and assignment of roles and judgement of validity. It is not only a matter of efficiency in the sense of lower costs, but also a matter of access to relations outside the clan or tribe, which greatly increases the variety of contacts and sources of new ideas, of novel combinations for innovation and learning.

However, it entails a loss of social contact and the intrinsic social value of relations, in ongoing give and take. It is a matter of transactions rather than relations. Also, contracts can never be complete, and unfamiliar situations can arise by surprise, and though giving stability and continuity, institutional fixtures can be circumvented and changed. In particular, especially relations of collaboration for innovation suffer from a paradox. On the one hand, the uncertainty of innovation yields a desire for security, but, on the other hand, there needs to be uncertainty in the form of room for exploration beyond the current order.

This requires reversion, to some extent, to social deliberation, not purely economic relations of give and take, in 'voice', and the exercise of trust. There, the social is again at play, in the giving of gifts without guaranteed commensurate return, and the collective, in the operation of reputation next to bilateral agreements and formal authority (Nooteboom 2002). It is difficult to switch back to social skills, which many, especially economists, find difficult to accept and muster, due to the 'inefficiency' and ambiguity of the social dynamics involved.

This social ability is a 'dynamic capability' to be added to those discussed in Chapter 1.

How about language? In language within a nation, everybody is connected to everybody else, except of course immigrants and expats, in the 'langue' discussed in the preceding chapter, leaving 'cracks' of personal meanings, in 'parole'.

Networks have increasingly gone across national boundaries, including language, with people learning other languages than their own, especially English. As they cross boundaries, the ties generally have less strength, in all of their dimensions of multiplexity, frequency of contact, continuity and investment. European integration means that people share more and more in networks across boundaries, with increasing density and strength. Hence the importance, among other things, of free movement across borders of people, knowledge and goods. But now, for some, that movement is seen not as a vehicle for identity but as a threat to it.

Does everyone want networks? Libertarians and inveterate loners do not want ties but absence of them, absence of interference, in an ideology of autonomy, free markets and minimal government, under the illusion that they are autonomous and can fend for themselves. And then they form tight groups among themselves, in defence of that ideology. That is more like the box again, without much need for contact, sharing some fixed perceived essence of being, with a few symbols to bind them, such as the flag and the myth of the rugged individual, the survivalist. With the loner one wonders whether this is a free choice or a withdrawal into resentment from feelings of disappointment and neglect, especially by people who feel excluded from networks of influence and power.

This uncovers a problem associated with the rise of populism. Populism on the right is associated with nationalism and, according to the container metaphor, this excludes Europeanism. You are in the nation, taken up in it, or you are outside. Nationalism is exclusive of outsiders, and is to be distinguished from patriotism which allows for networks across nations.

There is another factor, neglected, in particular, by economists, and by me, in the past. Economic doctrine demanded maximum flexibility, without obstacles to the flow of capital.

That neglected factor is that people have a natural urge to feel rooted in a local community, where they congregate in jobs, the pub after work, the church, community activities, sports, and mutual support and care. In the United States, for example, there was a strong tradition of such communities, with an ethic of decency and mutual support. These communities have mostly gone, torn apart by the economic logic of *comparative advantage*, according to which economic activity should take place where it is done more efficiently than other activities. The community is broken down by economies of scale, yielding a concentration of production in large firms, at increasing distance from where people live, yielding shopping malls not in the centre but at the periphery of municipalities, replacing small shops in villages and city quarters, with families moving away, fewer children and schools and consequent loss of local transport. This makes life harder for the elderly, yielding congregation in larger homes for their care.

These forces not only entailed a break-up of locality but also instability, with a focus on the short-term future. That discourages long-term investment and investments that are 'specific' to relations, needed for their quality, not only social quality but also economic quality of adding value in collaboration, with complementary competencies and mutual investment in relations and teams. Those even increase profit, in the production of specialties instead of low-margin mass products. But those investments require some stability, sufficient time to recoup them, make them worthwhile. One should seek not maximum but optimal flexibility: enough to prevent stagnation, but not so large as to discourage high-value relationships.

The highly educated – being more mobile, footloose, having access to more networks – could come along in the ensuing globalisation, surfing international networks. The lower educated and poor were left behind, in lesser access to networks, and were left alone in their isolation in crumbling communities, and this yielded a build-up of resentment. For them, identity is still the box they want to be in, but that box has emptied, fallen apart under the forces of globalisation, in cross-border networks. They now blame Europe for uprooting local communities and old values of family, religion and community. The people voting for Brexit want to get back to 'little England'.

There has been a widening divergence, with an increase of economic, cognitive, social, and cultural distance between the lower and the higher-educated and paid groups; between 'the people 'somewhere' and the 'nowhere people' connected in the cross-border networks.

Both national governments and European administration have focused on economic costs, on efficiency of flexibility, increase of scale, concentration and international trade, neglecting the social and political costs of losing locality.

Relations

As acknowledged by economists, exchange relations are needed for division of labour. Less recognised by them, relations are also needed for collaboration. As discussed above, they are also needed for cognitive development of the self, and economists don't recognise that. It was recognised already by Aristotle that the human being is a social or, as he called it, a 'political' animal. As also discussed above, and related to cognition, in language also one needs a discursive community.

Derrida used the notion of *differance* as a verb, in contrast with the noun 'difference', in the same way that 'résonance corresponds to résoner'. According to Hartmut Rosa, man craves and needs relations that are *resonant*, reciprocal, where one has effects on the world, generating feelings of 'self-efficacy', and undergoes effects from it in relationships, 'horizontally' with other people, 'vertically' with 'higher powers' of the state, society and God, and 'diagonally' with objects. Man can often not achieve this, in the ever faster drive (called *acceleration* by Rosa) towards collecting diverse resources, one's share of the world, to fill one's finite life, in competition with others, in reduced, 'mute', relationships, driven only by self-interest. Responsiveness, reciprocity and resonance get lost and postponed to retirement, at which point one has unlearned the potential for resonance that children do have and are not taught to develop. Relationships are felt be cold and indifferent. This is akin to Max Weber's disenchantment, Lukacs's 'reification' of people, Durkheim's 'anomie'. Rosa contrasts resonance to Axel Honneth's notion of 'recognition': Recognition may be needed, but is not all. It can be one-sided and too confirmatory. Resonance can be oppositional, like friends exerting criticism precisely because they are friends.

The analysis of Rosa is useful and fruitful, but I think there is more to it, that underlying resonance there is something more basic. In the pursuit of happiness, resonance – in interaction – is a means, not an end.

Relations can offer positive as well as negative power. Here I use the definition of power as the ability to affect choices of people. That can be negative, in constraining the options for choice, and imposing a choice among them. It can be positive in creating new options and leaving the choice open. New options arise from what different parties can offer each other, in products or competencies, with different forms of capital (knowledge, competence, position, access, means, etc.).

In relations, power can be negative as a result of dependence, especially when that is not symmetric, and the least dependent party can be tempted to put the other under pressure, taking his advantage in appropriating a larger share of jointly produced value. That supresses that other party if it cannot walk out because held up or because there is no alternative.

Earlier philosophers have focussed on the negative side of power, for example, Jean-Paul Sartre. In his play 'Huis Clos', he told of a threesome of people that derailed into hell, where they tortured each other, in shifting coalitions of two against one, to such an extent that punishment by hellfire was not needed: 'Hell, that is the others' (l'enfer, c'est les autres), he wrote. Admittedly, one can get overwhelmed or terrorised by others, but one can also see the other as an opportunity for supplementation and support. As discussed before, cognitive distance can have a benefit.

Dependence can arise from so-called specific investments in the relation, that is, investments that have value only within the relationship, and are lost when the relation breaks. It is especially such investments that make a relationship special, yield high added value. High quality and innovation often arise from combinations of different competencies, and that requires adjustment to each other by way of specific investments. Those can lie in buildings, machinery, tools and training, in finding the right people in the organisation one works with, and time and trouble taken in building trust. A relation must also last sufficiently long to recoup the investment, make it worthwhile.

The question then is how to deal, in 'governance', with the plusses and minuses of power. One possibility is to ensure that power is balanced. That can be done in striving for equal dependence with about the same amount of specific investments or shared ownership of them. One can also try to prevent misuse of power by means of control, with a contract or by way of a hierarchical relationship. The latter means that the one party takes over the other, brings it under its authority. Both approaches have their problems. Contracts can be slow, expensive and difficult to implement, when one has little monitoring and control of its execution. Especially under the uncertainty of innovation, it is difficult to know in advance what is to be allowed, to be put in the contract. Contracts can form a straitjacket that constrains innovation, disables constructive surprises and yields less of the motivation of autonomy. The imposition of particular actions takes away the flexibility of relationships. If one makes contracts they can, however, be procedural, indicating how to report and communicate, rather than specifying acts in the execution of a project.

Earlier, I indicated that the social skill in engaging in a fruitful relationship, combining complementary resources, is a dynamic capability, enhancing innovation. That is elaborated, in its conditions and procedure, in Chapter 5, including a discussion of how to manage trust in relations.

Integration under a shared hierarchy is an alternative to contracts, but that yields a convergence of ideas, views and modes of operation that diminishes the diversity, the cognitive distance that can be so fruitful.

How, then, can one reduce the risks of dependence between organisations without integration, maintaining maximum autonomy? That can be achieved with a motivation that keeps in check self-interest, resists opportunism, so that dependence is not immediately exploited, and values joint interest above self-interest, entailing some degree of altruism. Next to the instrumental value of the relationship it is also seen to have intrinsic value, value in the relationship itself, for which one is willing to surrender some revenue and one does not aim to scrape the bottom of the barrel. I will argue in the following paragraph how the human being was endowed by an inclination towards that in its evolution. The manifestation of it occurs more easily in collectivist societies than in individualistic ones.

In sum, in relationships one can try to reduce risks either by control, in contracts or hierarchy, or by trust and virtues. I recall that according to Harmut Rosa the human being has a thirst for resonance, mutual influence in relations. There is paucity of that in the social distance and pressure to stay at home imposed as a result of the corona crisis, causing distress.

On the other hand, according to a rule of thumb from sociology, the maximum size for a group of people to maintain its coherence on the basis of contact and reputation, enabled by personal contacts and gossip is about 150 people. Beyond that one needs hierarchy, or a shared ethic, often in the form of ideology.

A hierarchy can arise, among other things, from concentration of power in central positions. One kind of centrality is the number of direct ties a node has in a network, creating or withholding access. Here, there is a 'Matthew effect': the rich get richer. Having many contacts attracts new contacts. Another form of centrality, and also a source of power, lies in is *betweenness centrality*, the number of indirect ties that run through the node; the degree to which it constitutes a crossroad in the network. Such positional advantage channels contacts between people and is all the more important as sources of collective identity disappear, such as church, community or neighbourhood.

A political party is best seen not as box to which you belong or not, but as a network of leaders, producers of ideas, opinion makers and functionaries (ministers, parliamentarians, local administrators), with varying degrees of positional power, who contribute in different degrees to a shared ideology and style. Such a network with nodes of power harbours the danger of condensing into an elite that no longer fulfils the task of representing an electorate, which can lead to upheaval or desertion by which it fades away.

Next to hierarchy and positional power, and as the cement of the network, there is symbolic order that forms the tie between people, reinforcing the party's ideology. In his recent book on identity, Fukuyama spoke of 'credal identity': shared ideas on behaviour and belief on norms and habits. After the falling away of religion, common ethnicity and community, that is all we still have. However, that belief is not uniform. As in language, people attach different meanings to such normative ideas.

Symbols can take the form of icons and role models. The view of symbols can also change. Imperialist heroes to which statues were dedicated are now despicable colonialists. Sobriety was once seen as a trait of the Dutch, but now they spin off in emotion and hype.

Communities

On the one hand, there are forces of concentration of power in large countries, such as the United States and China, or associations of nations, as the EU. Such integration is needed for effective defense, foreign, monetary, and environmental policies. Among other things, only those large aggregates have the power to resist the huge platform companies (Google, Facebook, Amazon, etc.) in their capture of the infrastructure and processes of communication, and to affect global markets, free trade and geopolitics. On the other hand, there is a drive to decentralise politics and economies to regional and local communities, to bring them closer to citizens, allowing for more direct influence, partly to stem the rise of populism. There is some shrinking of extended networks from indirect ties to direct contacts. This will not eliminate all local inequalities, but one may hope for less exclusion. This can be assured by electing a local ombudsman. There are new opportunities for all kinds of local production, with 3D printing of all kinds of things, allowing for unique products, local energy production, with solar cells or windmills, and small-scale farming of produce, distributed through block chains. Local administrators and politicians are confronted directly with the effects of their policies, in contrast with distant national politicians. Firms are confronted directly with their environmental effects. Citizens are confronted with each other and can less afford, and are less inclined to, discrimination and exclusion.

Communities have been promoted as increasing equality in breaking down elites and hierarchies, decreasing exclusion and promoting voice, but inequality will increase between communities as they create custom-made arrangements, tailored to community composition and conditions.

In *restorative justice* (RJ), justice can be brought closer to the community. RJ is contrasted with criminal justice (CJ), in that while CJ is oriented mostly towards protection of society, beyond incarceration and retribution, RJ is oriented at rehabilitation of the perpetrator, reintroduction into society, and repair, restoration on the part of the victim. The focus of RJ is not to respond to harm with harm. Since offenses are often embedded in communities, RJ can also help to restore community relations, and there may be other participants in the process than offender and victim. The cause of offense often lies in faulty community relations, and the community can benefit from a good restoration.

The aim is for the offender to understand the harm inflicted, and his motivation for it, and to develop empathy and gain the insight and motivation to better himself, facilitating rehabilitation. The aim for the victim is to have the damage mended, not just material but also psychological damage, reducing stress, soothing the impulse at violent revenge, and perhaps achieving some forgiveness.

The meeting between offender, victim and community has no fixed scenario. It varies with the case and personal conditions. A key feature of a meeting is that it is voluntary. That requires some trust (British Home Office 1999). If the penalty for the offender has been established before a meeting, this may promote the trust that is needed. Involvement of a community may take the form of a conference. Not all communities are equally able to do this. It needs development and preparation. Punishment may take the form of community services. RJ by itself may not eliminate all possible power distance between offender and victim. A mediator may control this, but the scrutiny and intervention of a judge may be needed.

The advantages of RJ are primarily psychological, but there are also obvious economic and societal advantages of RJ: fewer expensive court sessions, less delay, hopefully less recidivism (repeat offending) and lower costs of prisons. However, it does involve cost in the form of time of offenders, victims and mediators, training, oversight to prevent power imbalances and unjust outcomes. However, the benefit of RJ is not so much extrinsic, in achieving such goals, but intrinsic, in improving the quality of the relationship and of society.

The empirical evidence is mixed. RJ works differently for different people. Overall, recidivism declined, more for crimes with personal harm than for property crimes; post-traumatic stress syndrome (PTSS) declined according to a survey by Sherman and Strang (2007) that compared many cases of RJ. C. J. Daly (2001) reported, in a study conducted on 170 young offenders in 1998 and 1999, that young offenders are more prone to promote their rehabilitation than restoration of the victim.

Beyond communities, there is still need for building on a national scale, of roads, rails, bridges, and part of health care, transport systems, laws and legal oversight, fights against criminality, and environmental policy. National oversight may be needed to prevent local clientism.

Chapter 5

MORALITY AND ETHICS

Institutions and Ethics

Are morals and institutions processes? Do they change? They do. In the first wave of corona there was solidarity and conformance to the rules, but in the second wave there has been rising rebellion from loss of individual freedom of movement and association. More generally, democratic ethics has declined, in increasing acceptance of authoritarian rule. Climate change requires a shift of virtues.

Institutions and ethics are needed to enable society. Hodgson (1998, 183) discussed the meaning of institutions. He reported Veblen's (2009, 239) definition of institutions as 'settled habits of thought common to the generality of men' and North's (1990, 3) definition as 'the rules of the game or [...] the humanly devised constraints that shape human interaction'. Let us here define institutions as humanly devised rules of the game and habits that guide human conduct. They are enabling constraints: they not only constrain but at the same time enable conduct. Richard Nelson once gave the example of a path through a swamp. It limits your steps, not to fall into the swamp, but it enables you to cross that swamp. Rules are, originally at least, explicit and conscious, but they can develop into habits. Habits can be and are often tacit or even unconscious, assimilated in education. They are not, however, instinctive, innate. Hodgson (1989, 179) characterised institutions as having five common characteristics: they involve interaction of agents, have common conceptions and routines, sustain and are sustained by shared conceptions and expectations, are relatively durable, incorporate values, and are seen as morally just.

Examples of rules are laws, as of property and the voluntary nature of trade, regulations of many kinds, including, say, traffic signs, but also language with its grammar and syntax. Organisations such as business firms are also institutions. I propose that next to institutions or as part of them, morality yields more informal rules for conduct in relations. I define ethics as the values and assumptions underlying morality. Ethics is the philosophy of morality.

Much of philosophy has been dedicated to finding a secure religious or other foundation for ethics and morality. Once it was God, but Feuerbach claimed that God was a diversion from man's own task of fixing ethics. According to another tradition, for Hobbes, the human being in its 'state of nature' was only oriented at self-interest and survival, leading to war of all against all, and an authority was needed to control it with laws and regulations with corresponding punishments. It is certainly true that self-interest is a strong force in the evolution of the human being, to promote survival and reproduction. But is there more to motivation?

A third stream in the history of ideas is that people have an innate inclination towards benevolence and forbearance. How could that have arisen? In the evolution of humanity, it was advantageous for survival to collaborate, in defence and foraging, and this was helped by the capacity for empathy, putting oneself in the shoes of the other, to see what he needed for collaboration, and to engage in signalling and some sort of communication. It has led to a widely felt principle of reciprocity: you are supposed to return a favour, sooner or later.

Justice arose as also needed for the viability of a community. This was a matter of self-interest, to sustain a society; however, in contrast with institutions, that also may have developed into an innate drive, an instinct, because of its adaptive value in evolution. An alternative to being innate is that it is internalised, becoming a habit, in education, schooling and practice.

Why do we need morality as an unwritten part of institutions, and ethics beyond that? Why do institutions not suffice? Many institutions are written, formal, or take the form of organisations with an institutional task, such as the police and the judiciary. They also entail mostly negative power, indicating what we are forbidden to do. Much of morality and all of ethics are not rules but habits: voluntary and subject to personal conviction and interpretation, and offer a direction where one might go. That is oriented to positive power, enabling people, and gives more freedom, room for authenticity. The more morality and ethics are pursued, the fewer explicit rules one needs.

Traditionally, liberalism has rejected public moral debate, seeing morality and ethics as a private affair, not to be meddled with by the state. But ethics as a voluntary guidance of behaviour can reduce the need for rules, thus allowing for more individual liberty. The wariness of public moral debate has been ascribed to the view, when liberalism arose in the seventeenth century, after disastrous religious wars, that morality is a matter of religion, and to prevent the wars from happening again, it was best to leave morality and ethics as a private, not public affair (Copleston 1964–67). This has given business a powerful excuse to dodge ethics: it is not their business to engage in morality, which is seen as paternalistic or even undemocratic. Morality has shrunk to 'compliance' with rules, often as a cosmetic device. However, in present times there are again excesses of unethical behaviour yielding injustice and inequality, which call for public debate and inclusion of ethics in education and training, not to impose any particular ethics, but to generate awareness of the options and arguments for them. Much thought has gone into them in 2,500 years of philosophy and scientific experiments, in child research, game theory and anthropology, and it would be unwise not to take them into account. In any case we are involved in thoughts and discussions of ethics in daily life, mostly implicitly, in the raising of children, relations of marriage, family, friendship and community, and are confronted with ethical issues in literature, films, series on TV and news. It would be playing hide and seek to ignore it, and foolish not to make use of the thought that has gone into it.

However, there have been objections to morality. Bernard de Mandeville claimed that there is little evidence of virtue and that a society endowed with all the virtues would be a static, stagnant society (Copleston 1964–67, vol. 5, part I, 188). Private vices, such as egotism, are public virtues. Virtues might suppress initiative and thymos, the drive and spirit of life, too much, which can harm both the individual, taking away the gist of life, and render society pallid and dull, as de Mandeville suggested.

Nietzsche (2013) claimed that virtues such as pity and charity are a ploy from the will to power of the weak and suppressed, to control and to exert vengeance on the strong and dominant. The problem with that dominance, for the strong themselves, is that it leads to a self-centred, solipsist ethics. Nietzsche's stance is not viable because the individual is social, constituted in relations with others, and needs the opposition of the other to clear preconceptions. (Nooteboom 2012).

As an Aristotelian, I seek an intermediate position between extremes: we need morality and virtues, but with restraint. That is why I am careful to stress personal choice in weighing ethical injunctions, avoid their formal forms and do not see them as uniformly imposed duties A problem is that moral choices are often presented as self-evident while they are based on tacit ideologies, hiding power and inequalities, as shown by Michel Foucault, Pierre Bourdieu and others. Such obfuscations are not always malevolent. People are inevitably guided by hidden, taken-for-granted assumptions. I adopted the definition of power as affecting choice. That can be done in a negative, restraining way, reducing options and imposing choice, but also in a positive way, widening options and leaving choice open. The latter makes for greater uncertainty and 'choice stress', and is therefore sometimes avoided. Restrictions would evoke censure when overt, and to hide this, a choice is presented ideologically as unavoidable and self-evidently needed. This arises from the condition that human capacity for rational attention is limited, and the pressure of circumstance forces speedy decisions. Much is therefore chosen unreflectively, by routine, habit and indoctrination, raising obstacles to authenticity.

A Brief History

Ethics concerns the purpose of life. What is that purpose? Here, I adopt the view from the pragmatist philosopher John Dewey (in the nineteenth and twentieth centuries) that the purpose of life is spiritual growth of man, in realising his potential, in a balance of material pleasure and spiritual well-being, in response to the exigencies of life, solving problems. My definition of the good life is as follows: contributing to something greater than yourself, and if you do this with maximal development and use of your talents it is pleasurable. This is a process view, in contrast to the goal of life as some eternal, fixed, Platonic, absolute good. I would find that suffocating. My maxim is 'imperfection on the move': one will never achieve perfection, but improvement is possible. What succeeds, in pragmatic adaptation, depends on the uncertain and unpredictable contingencies of life. The pragmatic intention to deal with those is not always successful. There are numerous examples in history where thought and societal conditions deteriorated, often disastrously, due to unintended consequences of decisions. That is happening, with a vengeance, in current society. Dewey's claim presupposes a criterion of progress and regress. What is the measure of it? I claim that this lies in ethics, in particular virtues that one strives to see fulfilled. Let us take a step back in the history of ideas.

Most thinkers in the history of philosophy held that human beings are primarily motivated by self-interest but also have a moral sense. In the seventeenth to the eighteenth century, Shaftesbury and Hutcheson held that people are naturally social, with a moral sense. Hutcheson claimed that 'by the moral sense we perceive pleasure, in the contemplation of good actions in others, and are determined to love the agent (and much more do we perceive pleasure in being conscious of having done such actions ourselves) without any view of further natural advantage from them' (Copleston 1964–67, 190). It is not clear whether Hutcheson meant, as an object of 'pleasure', the actions or the underlying virtues.

In the seventeenth century, David Hume had postulated an innate instinct for benevolence, regardless of utility, and justice as a more utilitarian, what he called 'artificial', principle needed for a viable society (Copleston 1964–67, vol. 5, part II, 131, 40; Stroud 1977 216–17). The puzzle in his philosophy then is why people honour rules of justice even if that is to their disadvantage, when they can avoid punishment or loss of reputation. The only solution I can see is that this virtue is inculcated in education and practice, turning it into an often subconscious habit, or as an instinct, in the genes, acquired in the evolution of humanity, to become as natural and innate as benevolence. It becomes part of the person one wants to be. If it is in the genes, this would raise the puzzle that the advantage is to society, while genes are individual, and the temptation would still be to cheat and gain advantage in evolutionary selection, whereby selfish genes would in the end prevail. I will return to that puzzle presently.

Even Macchiavelli, in the fifteenth century, who had pleaded for an opportunistic, devious, lying, cheating monarch, admitted that this does not apply to the population at large, since that would disable a viable society. However, David Hume warned that an 'ought' is not an 'is'. Yet, the 'is' of survival in evolution can have developed into an innate 'ought'.

The key question is how to define what is good. What is the purpose of morality? A recent tradition that I follow (Moseley 2019; Tomasello 2016) is that morality served humanity in its evolution, during 400,000 years, mostly in small tribes of hunter-gatherers. For survival, people needed each other and became interdependent, and this required morality. This started with building an ability to conduct specific joint projects such as defence and hunting big game, in dedicated mutual support, and then, as communities grew, relations became wider and more impersonal, in a variety of cooperation, and it became inefficient to build up dedicated relations of mutual understanding and forbearance each time, separately for each project, and a generalised ability to cooperate developed (Tomasello 2016).

There is a puzzle here that frequently recurs in debates. If collaboration is needed for survival, the morality needed for it is said to shrink to self-interest, and utilitarian philosophers and economists say that there really is nothing beyond self-interest. But while morality and altruism are useful in the long run, the proximate cause, in the short run, is genuine other-directedness and altruism, possibly yielding sacrifice. They are adaptive, but that is not necessarily the motive for them. I do not help people because it is good for society but because I think it is a good thing to do. Of course, morality competes with self-interest also in the short term, as a proximate cause, in the form of individual survival and pleasure, which often is stronger than ethics and wins out. The point here is that other-interest does exist and sometimes does win. MacIntyre (2011) distinguished between 'external and internal' goods. External goods lie in the utility of a certain conduct, its instrumental value, in its outcome, such as money, fame, power, position or respectability. Internal goods lie in the intrinsic value of an activity in some field, as in sports, arts, science and healthcare.

Virtues may support or to some extent replace institutional rules, making them more viable. For example, in the Netherlands the maximum speed on all roads has been set at 100 kilometres per hour. Some people have already announced that they will not abide by the rule. Others will do so, supported by a conviction of the need to protect the environment. Without that, the limit would not work. It would require too much control and sanction. Currently, in the Netherlands there is a debate whether obligatory quarantine for corona-infected can be imposed legally, and is not in conflict with constitutional law. It would be better to inculcate it as a civic virtue.

In the eighteenth/nineteenth century, Jeremy Bentham, father of *Utilitarianism*, was a follower of the *hedonist* Epicurus, in founding human conduct exclusively on the enhancement of pleasure and avoidance of pain, but like most utilitarians he was committed to the commonality of man, with the most pleasure and least pain for as many people as possible. He granted that the human being has empathy by association: seeing people suffering, one imagines oneself in that position.

John Stuart Mill was a follower of Bentham, but he went beyond him in claiming that the human being is not by nature purely selfish. His argument was that pleasures are not all of the same sort. Mental or spiritual pleasures are not the same as material ones, and can differ not only in quantity but also in quality. They have intrinsic value, regardless of any instrumental utility.

Intellectually, this is disastrous for the habit and purpose that is characteristic of orthodox, mainstream economics, to maximise a utility function (Hodgson 2019), which has the implicit claim that all pleasures are commensurable, can be subsumed in the same utility function. As Milbank and Pabst (2016, 130) put it, 'more intangible goals of community belonging, work satisfaction, and aspirations for cultural richness and beauty are set aside'. I add: the intrinsic value of morals and ethical principles is not commensurable with their utility. J. S. Mill made an important step in recognising that not all values are of the same kind. Spiritual satisfaction is not the same as material consumption. Virtue may yield material sacrifice, so that one value is to be sacrificed for another, and utility functions are not independent between people since they include censure of conduct and reputation. J. S. Mill also saw the human being as a social animal. In fact, that goes back to Aristotle, who saw that community was needed for the individual to realise its potential. That has great consequences for economics, in the need to bring in sociology and anthropology.

It is difficult to decide whether certain virtues are innate or acquired in education and practice in the world and adjustment to censure. There is, however, an evolutionary argument that some virtues are innate or virtually innate, which means that the human being has an innate capability of developing them in experience. That applies also to fear: one has an inborn proclivity to fear, but whether this is fear of snakes, spiders or snakes depends on one's environment. Here, the notion of *prewiring* of the brain, or *virtual innateness* is useful: we inherit not specific, determinate features, but the potential to develop them in interaction with the environment, for optimal adaptiveness. That helps in the well-known controversy of 'nature vs. nurture'. How else can we reconcile them, in the effects of both?

Groups, of kinship or tribe, were internally helpful and solidary with each other and at the same time engaged in vociferous warfare with rival groups, in the fight for resources. Their solidarity was based on mutual acquaintance and recognition. This is elaborated in the notion of *parochial altruism* (de Dreu et al. 2014). That is the phenomenon that people are inclined to altruism within the group they feel to be a member of, while mistrusting outsiders. That yields an evolutionary puzzle. It is conducive to trust and solidarity within the group, but genes are owned by the individual, not the group. The hazard for a trusting society is that it will be invaded by opportunist outsiders who ultimately gain ascendance, due to better individual survival. It is true, as demonstrated in the game of *hawk and dove*, that after a while, when the number of collaborators (doves) dwindles, the opportunists (hawks) begin to lose out on victims, and a balance between collaborators and opportunists may arise, and not all collaborators die out. But mistrust, identification and punishment of outsiders, with altruistic punishment by a sufficient number, at a cost to themselves, is a remedy to maintain a wider society of cooperators. Tragically, here lies the source of discrimination and exclusion of certain immigrants.

Parochial altruism hampers the positive value of diversity, as a source of a variety of scarce resources, in exchange, but there is more to it. Thought is always biased, and the best opportunity one has of escaping that bias is opposition from someone else with a different slant on things. That is why diversity is good for innovation as well as intellectual and spiritual development.

The solution to the discrimination and exclusion resulting from parochial altruism is to extend the boundary of the group one considers oneself to be a member of, as living in the same neighbourhood, for example, or trying to categorise the outsider by some other feature, such as a colleague at work, sharing a sport or task, or being the victim of the same hardship or injustice. Here again, networks are a better model for identity than the 'container metaphor'.

Parochial altruism goes together with group self-serving attributions, where positive properties or actions outside the group are attributed to circumstances, not properties, and negatives are attributed to personal characteristics, while inside the group it is the reverse.

Stereotypes are convenient for people as cognitive shortcuts to categorisation of others and for dealing with them. Those trigger a 'frame' for perception and action are discussed elsewhere. They are also used for differentiating their groups from other groups along dimensions that yield favorable comparisons.

A key dimension identified in all ethnic or cultural stereotypes of character, however, is the "beneficence" dimension, involving such traits as being honest, kind, loyal and trustworthy' (Smith and Bond 1993, 179, 86).

In contrast with the utilitarian ethics of Bentham and followers, another system is the deontological or duty ethics of Immanuel Kant. While utilitarianism looks only at outcomes, in terms of utility, Kantian ethics disregards outcomes, in principle, and looks at intentions. Best known is the 'categorical imperative': Follow only the maxim (guidance of behaviour) that you would like to be a universal rule, applying always to everyone, as a new version of the ancient 'Golden Rule' that arose in the 'axial age' between 900 and 200 BC, in Hinduism, Buddhism, Jewish monotheism, Taoism and Confucianism, proclaiming that 'one should (not) do onto others that one (does not) want(s) done to oneself'. Here we again have the puzzle why people would always practice such a rule, when it may have disadvantages to themselves. An example is lying to escape a predicament. This is not an innate principle but a matter of rationality. If the consequence is useful or pleasurable, that is a bonus, but not the reason for doing it, according to Kant. I find that difficult to accept, because in my view what you should do or not depends on the situation. I might lie to save a life or not insult someone. Nevertheless it is impressive in that reason conquers the impulse of desire, and in that sense it is a manifestation of freedom. Another is virtue ethics, going back to Aristotle, but also going beyond him.

Virtues

Of the main systems of ethics, such as utility ethics, duty ethics and virtue ethics, I opt for Aristotelian virtue ethics. Virtues are the nuts and bolts of ethics, as inclinations, character traits. The classic, central, 'cardinal' virtues, around which everything turns (cardinality) are prudence, courage, moderation and justice. They are general, applying across many cultures and nations. There are many more virtues, more specific to a culture, profession, location or condition. Aristotle even mentioned humour as a virtue (Aristotle 1999, 68).

Like other evaluations, ethical judgement is partly habitual, even subconscious, in a compromise between efficiency and the quality of judgement (Woo 1992, 6.). Of the four classical virtues, reason or reasonableness is needed for everything else. How destructive irrationality can be shows up, for example, in surprisingly widespread conspiracy theories. Courage, a second virtue, is needed to accept the risk and uncertainties of activity and relationships, and to accept the vulnerability of trust. That is needed to sustain your role as someone on whom reliance can be placed, as part of friendship, accepting the risk of harm in extending care and concern (MacIntyre 2011, 123). I have argued (Nooteboom 2019a) that, in contrast with economists who claimed that trust is not viable under the competition in markets and is to be reserved for personal relations of family and friends (Williamson 1993), trust is necessary in markets, as a leap of faith (Moellering 2009) to engage in relations, which are most uncertain when they aim to connect complementary competencies, for the sake of quality or innovation. Trust is part of the dynamic capability of engaging in relations, profiting from complementary capabilities or other assets, discussed before.

The virtue of moderation is required to give some room in income and wealth to others than the rich, and in view of the diminishing returns for the rich. Other virtues are more or less related to the four main ones. Telling the truth, for example, is related to reason; self-control and patience are related to moderation; friendliness to justice; moderation, resilience and perseverance to courage; and hospitality, generosity and magnanimity to justice.

For Aristotle, ethics is a practical affair, with *phronesis*, a judgement that takes into account ever variable conditions, allowing for no strict Platonic universals. All ethical actions have the goal of happiness, some have a proximate goal of utility, in producing happiness, some have intrinsic value of happiness, a value in themselves, such as playing music. Likewise, Aristotle also added the intrinsic, internal good to the external, the merely utilitarian.

Virtues and their enactment should refer to life as a whole, called *eudaimonia*, in a process of development, in which one is constituted, in becoming the person one wants to be, not an accumulation of happy moments of pleasure. As a result, virtues fit in a story, a narrative, of one's life (MacIntyre 2011 210). Life is to be lived in the awareness and acceptance of death. Heidegger talked of 'being unto death' (Sein zum Tode). From the perspective of death there is an incentive to not postpone good actions, but engage in them now.

There has been an effort, in the history of ideas, to find absolute, universal and fixed Platonic ethics and virtues, applying everywhere, under all circumstances and for everybody. The fear of relativisation, the lack of such universals, is that it may derail in arbitrariness, excuses, self-interest and special interests. Sympathy can derail into corruption.

In the evolution of humanity, cooperation, corresponding interdependence and its attendant morality is a universal, to the point that next to variety generation, selection and transmission, cooperation now seems to become a fourth principle of evolution, in the emerging field of sociobiology, or biosociology, or evolutionary sociology. The innate disposition towards trust, at least within groups, fairness, and forbearance, inherited from evolution, discussed before, is universal, except for sociopaths and psychopaths. That does however entail a general disposition that assumes different forms in different circumstances of culture, location and climate.

Universal also seems to be the golden rule. The cardinal virtues of reason, courage, moderation and justice also are fairly general if not universal. However, more widely, the absolute, the universal, is an illusion. The specifics of ethics depend on culture, on circumstances and on the individual and his profession, and those change in time, as shown in anthropological literature (Liisberg et al. 2015). As said before, moral sense is largely pre-wired, yielding specific forms as a function of circumstance. One may have several, conflicting obligations, necessitating a choice. It depends on profession. A doctor has different virtues from an architect.

There are great differences between philosophers, in different times and also concurrently, with different views concerning the role of virtues, the list of virtues and their rank order, even in the West, even when not including Eastern or Native American views (MacIntyre 2011). A theoretical argument is that virtues serve the good life, and different societies have different views on that. In Homeric times, virtues concerned good conduct according to one's social position, such as father of a family, soldier, athlete, ruler. There still is some of that, in the ethics peculiar to professions. With Aristotle, virtues concerned good conduct as a member of the Athenian polis. There are virtues of a good Christian. One imbues the virtues considered salient in upbringing, education, practice of a profession and so on.

As discussed before, in Chapter 4, there are differences between cultures. A prime example is differences, in many respects, between individualist and collectivist cultures. There are general, one is inclined to say 'universal', principles, as discussed earlier, but when one looks at how those are acted out in behaviour, differences emerge. There are similarities in the ability and drive to develop virtues. And some of the virtues, such as the four cardinal virtues, are quite general and widespread. Everyone favours the use of reason, in prudence and being reasonable, and justice, although the issue always is, in the opposition between political right and left, whether this is justice in the form of deserts, with low taxes, or of needs, with higher taxes and the distribution of income. Associated with this, views vary on the desirability of moderation and courage, with some people and cultures valuing security more. The variation also appears in the professions and careers that people choose.

My view is largely Aristotelian (Aristotle 1999), but not completely. Aristotle, following Plato, held that there can be no conflict between virtues. I think that there can be, for example, between the virtues of courage and justice, when a courageous entrepreneur creates an innovation that fails, causing damage in the form of loss of capital and employment. For another example, consider the scientist who feels compelled to go for the reputational good of highly cited, often fashionable publications, in order to earn time for research and a career, more than to go for the internal goods of contributing to insight and enjoying the pleasure of that and of the skills needed for it, and the challenge involved. One may have conflicting loyalties, as between job and family, and exigencies of circumstances. Suppose you are walking along a canal, with your little daughter by your hand. You see someone drowning and feel you should dive to the rescue, but you are wary to leave your daughter on the slippery slope.

Second, I think that some relevant virtues are missing in Aristotle, such as the Christian virtues of forgiveness and charity, faith, hope and love. Love here is love of people in general, 'agape', rather than desire (eros) or philia (loving friendship).

Also, one should keep in mind Mandeville's warning that virtues might suppress initiative and thymos too much, which can harm society. Thymos, as discussed before, is the urge to manifest oneself. It is also called 'conatus', and considered by some to be the main driver of conduct. It forms the gist of life and should not be eliminated.

As noted before, Nietzsche (2013) claimed that virtues such as pity and charity, are a ploy from the will to power of the weak and suppressed to control and to take vengeance on the strong and dominant. The problem with that is, however, that it leads to a fully self-centred, solipsist ethics. That, I argued (Nooteboom 2002), is not viable because the individual is social, constituted in relations with others. All knowledge is partial. One needs the views of others to complement and correct one's own view.

In sum, while the disposition towards morality and some ethical principles are universal, specific virtues are multiple and varied, and depend on culture, personal perspective of the good life, profession and circumstance. They can serve as a support or as a complement to institutional rules. Their advantage is that unlike the duty of rules they can be voluntary, appealing to conviction. They are not to be imposed but argued, with options to be taught in education and training.

If institutions and virtues guide behaviour, let us see how they play a role in a causality of behaviour, and how different these roles are. Bergson (1969, 73) distinguished three types of causality: impulse, triggering and unfolding. The efficient cause gives an impulse, like hitting a billiard ball, or pushing a door. One can trigger an explosion of dynamite with a flame. One unfolds music on a gramophone by playing a disc.

Economic Virtue

Economic virtues are the following. Markets enable division of labour and exchange of products needed for welfare, to have food and be healthy. The downside of it, its humanitarian damage, is shown where production and consumption are unequal. This manifests itself, in particular, in the corona crisis, with the inequality of access to medicine, hospitals and housing that allows for keeping distance and practising quarantine. We need markets, but we need to correct their many imperfections. The underlying virtues intended by economists, imperfectly realised, are freedom of choice, in production and consumption, equality of access to markets, without exclusion, the most efficient use of 'local' knowledge of desires and opportunities and capabilities, as argued by Friedrich von Hayek. Hayek called competition a 'discovery process', which contributes to the process view pursued in this book. What I also consider a virtue is the opportunity for people to incur risk and accept challenge in entrepreneurship and exercise what earlier I called 'thymos', the vitality of life, in the enjoyment of it and the demonstration of it, in a similar way that sports exemplify bodily thymos, science exemplifies intellectual thymos and art creative thymos.

However, the imperfections of markets are extensive and increasing, in limits to competition, in monopoly and oligopoly, and concentration in big firms, the attendant flight from taxes, power play in the lobbying for favourable taxes, subsidies, subsidised energy, low cost and quality of labour conditions, lax environmental regulation and control, discrimination and so-called transaction costs in evaluating differences in product quality or conditions.

Is this idea of lobbying a conspiracy theory? Earlier I argued against conspiracy theories, but conspiracies do exist, although it is a bit of a misnomer when the 'conspiracy' is at times tacit, non-deliberative, habitual and institutionalised. The important point is that as any theory it should observe the 'warrants' of theory, such as facts, logic and practical viability, and seek falsification.

An urgent political problem, getting attention at present, concerns the so-called platform companies, such as Google, Facebook, Twitter and Amazon, which operate in the public sector of information and communication that used to be a government affair, controlled by democracy, and are huge monopolies that atrophy capitalism, tailoring information about choice behaviour of citizens down to the level of individuals and sell it for marketing and even electoral purposes, moulding conduct. With this, we are moving away from the familiar arrangement of industrial society, with a division of labour between government, in a public sector, and private enterprise, in markets, and a balance of power between capital and labour (De Wit and Meyer 2017). With the use of information and communication technology and algorithms, labour becomes less central, and capital gains the upper hand. This is in accordance with Maalouf's account of the decline ('shipwreck' he called it)' of societies all over the world, particularly since the conservative revolution around 1979, discussed before.

The question is how governments can and should respond. One vile option is to collaborate with those companies in developing new technologies of monitoring and control of citizens. This is intensified as a result of the corona crisis, with an increased pressure to monitor conduct. The platform companies are eager to collaborate, to extend their profit potential and monopoly power, and some governments are tempted to collude in developing extended control, as already operational in China, with next to monitoring through the Internet and smartphones, the proliferation of cameras in public spaces, with facial recognition attached to them, developed into citizen's scores that give access, or refuse it, to public services, resulting in totalitarianism. The more beneficial alternative is to resist those companies and defend democracy (De Wit and Meyer 2017). An example is the intention of the EU to subject the platform companies to tax in the country where they generate profits, which is resisted by President Trump. One may be tempted to introduce a tax on the use of information, but one has to take care not to damage science and the information search and discourse for citizens. The solution is to tax the use of information when used for profit-making. Another measure is to restrict the ownership of user data to the user, and let the platform company pay for it.

Transaction costs, mentioned before, are, among other costs, the costs or limitations in fully judging the value of a product or service, their negative features, the truth of beneficial ones, reliability and creditworthiness of a customer, the cost of drawing up a contract or other agreement, the monitoring and control of its execution, haggling over interpretations and unforeseen conditions, costs of litigation, and costs of dedicated investments lost in a breakdown of the relation.

Bruni and Sugden (2008, 2013) made a useful distinction between benefit as an outcome of exchange, not necessarily intended as beneficial to the trading partner, but based purely on self-interest, and benefit intended ex ante, in an orientation towards being useful to the partner. They pleaded for the latter, in what they called 'fraternity'. That rhymes with the notion that the human being has an instinct towards collaboration, bred by the need for it in evolution, requiring interest and empathy, in imagining oneself in the shoes of the partner, to anticipate his needs and support. It rhymes also with Rosa's plea for 'resonance'.

Bruni and Sugden (2013, 154) asked whether the mutual benefit concerns the parties to market transactions or mutual benefit for everyone in society. There is no long-term legitimacy for business if it does not contribute to the flourishing of people and society.

Table 1 Sources of intentional reliability

	OUTSIDE	INSIDE
		US →
CONTROL	*narrowing the room for conduct* (institutions) contract *affecting choice of conduct* reputation	hierarchy, directives, incentives hostages
TRUST	general trust, morality, ethics	private trust: family, clan, friendship, community, empathy
		↓ Japan

Source: Nooteboom (2002).

As discussed before, in more developed societies, many relations are impersonal and transactional, and the basis for it is institutionalised, in property law, laws of exchange, formal appointments, membership of institutions and educational degrees. That has advantages of efficiency but entails that relations are transactional, impersonal. That can yield not only gain of efficiency but also loss of the intrinsic value of the relation. An example is transactional leadership, where acts are evaluated according to formal agreements laid down in contracts and rules, and inspiration and motivation are lost. Another example is an alliance of firms for pooling resources for innovation. The transactional mode, in legal or hierarchical control, can form a straitjacket, with no room for improvisation and deviation essential for innovation. Damage can be done to relations of friendship, marriage and parenthood. This can yield the loss of 'resonance' that Helmut Rosa notes. The lesson is that rules and formal agreements may at times be taken with a grain of salt, with some leeway, and as something to fall back on in case of need, and not as the primary guidance of conduct.

Reliance and Trust

Trust is emotional but can to some extent be rational, reflective, as opposed to an automatic, tacit, innate inclination to trust, at least within the group one feels to belong to. It can also be based on a rational analysis of why people might be trustworthy. Trust is, or should be, less about having trust and more about being trustworthy. This is illustrated in Table 1.

In the left half of the table one finds public factors, outside the relationship, and on the right factors within the relationship. In the top half of the table one finds control. This has two forms: affecting the room for action, by contract (outside the relationship) or hierarchy and incentives (inside the relationship), and affecting the choice of action within that space, by reputation, outside the relation (on the golf course, for example), or incentives inside the relation. In the top left one finds contracts, on the basis of the institution of the law, and other regulations by public institutions, such as government, education and professional media. The drawbacks of contracts is that they take time and can be costly and can signal distrust which calls forth reciprocal distrust, which once settled is difficult to remove. That is not necessarily the case, since the contract may be devised for technical reasons, not to prevent opportunism, but to document who is to do what, for planning purposes (Klein Woolthuis et al. 2005). In the top left one also finds reputation. Reputation is a matter of self-interest: one behaves well not to ruin the chance of a fruitful relation in the future, with the present partner or another. It requires a reputation mechanism, implemented by some intermediary such as the bookkeeper, or an industry association that is considered to be trustworthy in its competence to judge, to separate gossip from true reports, and in its intention to do so fairly. The current rise of conspiracy theories is due, in part, to loss of trust in institutions.

In the top right of the table one finds the institution of organisation, with a hierarchy, issuing directives and giving incentives, and the instrument of hostages, defined as something of value to the hostage giver but not the hostage taker, so that the latter will not hesitate to destroy the hostage when its giver does not honour obligations. It is an ancient instrument, with kings giving nobles from the court or family members as hostages. Now it can take the form of competition-sensitive information that can be divulged.

Beyond control by institutions and incentives, there is trust, beyond self-interest, based on ethics, outside the relation, in general trust, as a matter of culture, concerning the 'generalised other' (Mead 2011), or inside the relation, as a private bonding on the basis of (extended) family, clan, friendship or love.

I have considered the use of the concept of 'reciprocity'. On the one hand, it comes close to mutual help and collaboration, the 'mutual interest' that I used, in Table 1. On the other hand, reciprocity can also entail revenge, mutual harm, which is not intended in the table. It can deteriorate in harsh 'give and take', 'quid pro quo', in 'enlightened self-interest', that belongs more in the top row of the table, on control. What is intended here is the intention to help the other: to provide what you think is good for him or her, and make more or less significant compromises on the external value of profit or income. However, it is not friendship or 'fraternity', proposed by Bruni and

Sugden (2008). They presented that as an alternative to Adam Smith's separation of the private, in family and friendship and market contacts, presented as morally neutral transactions. I agree up to a point with Bruni and Sugden, but to me, friendship is more personal and private, and belongs in the right-bottom quadrant of the table. The 'fraternity' promoted by Bruni and Sugden belongs, I think, in the bottom left, equivalent to 'generalised trust'.

Bruni and Sugden present the following example: As a salesperson in a hardware store, would you tell a potential customer that for his purpose there is a cheaper alternative to the apparatus you have on offer, by another provider? The principle of intending to help would tell you to do that. Another example is from my wife. She went out with her daughter to profit from a special offer of a wooden floor. She went to the wrong shop. The salesperson demonstrated that in the special offer elsewhere certain additional costs and inconveniences had not been included, and that his product, though more expensive, did not have those drawbacks and in all was more advantageous. He argued out of self-interest but also, assuming that he was telling the truth, in the interest of the customer.

As discussed before, the evolution of humanity has bred an instinctive feeling for collaboration, with give and take, with an inclination towards benevolence, but this competes with an instinct of self-preservation that is also engendered in evolution. This is not a matter of either-or: one can value both the intrinsic and the extrinsic value of a job or relationship (Nelson 2009).

A sacrifice, in accepting less monetary reward, in a job or relationship, may also be due to its intrinsic value, of one's job satisfaction, conviction or relational quality. This may lead to the principle 'pay less and get more', where intrinsic valuation is seen as yielding a higher quality, of work or relationship, and can be obtained with a lower reward, as in teaching and healthcare or care for the elderly, handicapped or children. This may be seen as a form of exploitation.

As also argued by Nelson, intrinsic value includes not only the pleasure one may have in the job, such as technical challenge or social contact, but also the realisation of one's sense of life, in fulfilling a conviction or ideal, such as preserving the environment. It is odd, and contradictory, and can be counterproductive, to ask for a monetary, extrinsic reward for intrinsic motivation.

Table 1 can be used for the diagnosis of a relation, seeing what sources of trustworthiness are absent and present, and for therapy, seeking to add new sources of reliability. There is also the possibility of go-betweens (Nooteboom 2002). They can serve to break through emotional deadlocks, and put deliberation on a more sober, rational track than the emotional suspicions that often accompany relations. Relations are often governed by unjustified suspicions, especially in case of the 'Calimero's Syndrome' of a small, vulnerable partner, who is overly suspicious because of it, residing in a 'loss frame', expecting and seeing opportunism everywhere. The go-between can relieve unjust suspicions. He can advise on how to proceed in deliberation. He can serve as a guarantor or monitor, instead of a contract. This may have the advantage of the go-between safekeeping sensitive information, rather than divulging it in a contract, with the risk of it 'spilling over'. Trust is an ongoing process, and needs to be guarded against undue suspicion and misunderstandings.

The analysis helps to understand the difference between reliance and trust. Table 1 shows the sources of intentional reliability, outside and inside the relationship. Reliability can be based on control or on trustworthiness beyond control.

The scheme can also be used to understand differences between countries. It has been used, for example, for a comparison of trust between the United States and Japan (Nooteboom 2019b). In the United States, trust is largely based on contract and reputation. One of its disadvantages is that it is expensive, yielding high transaction costs, and slow, in the building of a contract and reputation. As Fukuyama (1995) claimed, the United States has low generalised trust. But while he also claimed that Japan is a 'high trust society', the Japanese researchers Yamagishi and Yamagishi (1994) showed that generalised trust in Japan is low. There, relationships in business are largely based on hierarchy and bonding in family and clans. In the Netherlands, I think, all sources are in play, with hierarchy being relatively weak. In both Japan and the Netherlands, American governance is being adopted more than in the past, in a juridification of relations, in contracts and litigation.

There is a positive bias in trust, as if it is always a good thing. But trust can go too far, in several ways:

- Trust in untrustworthy people is misplaced. If trust decreases because trustworthiness decreases, that is a good thing.
- Blind trust: in disregarding the possibility or evidence of a lack of trustworthiness.
- Trust out of desperation: there is no alternative. This connects to Albert Hirschman's recognition of 'loyalty' next to 'voice' and 'exit'. If there is no basis for deliberation, in voice, and no option of exit, in being pinned down or coerced, there is only one option of staying put and making the best of it. In Russia under Stalin, people talked lovingly of 'little father' Stalin, in spite of his blatant terror. Psychologically, it was unbearable to face reality.
- The disadvantage of bonding in family or clan, as indicated for Japan, is that relationships are locked into such clans, excluding variety from outside, which can be bad for innovation.

- One can have multiple, conflicting obligations, to job, family, personnel, customers, suppliers, environment, nation, that necessitate disloyalty to at least one, in a crisis, and one can be untrustworthy there by necessity.
- According to the philosopher Nietzsche, benevolence and pity are the result of the power play of the weak to protect them against the strong or exert vengeance on them.
- According to Bernard Mandeville, private vices are public virtues. I would say that the duty of benevolence can eliminate the virtuous power of 'Thymos', the urge to excel and perform of the entrepreneur, discoverer, sportsman, scientist and the like.

However, one can be honest in some of those conflicts, ask for sympathy, offer recompense, or accept retribution. One can be trustworthy in one's untrustworthiness.

Concerning the process of trust, there are questions how to start, but also how to maintain a relationship and, certainly not less important, how to end a relationship in reasonably good faith. Suppose the partner is unknown, so that reputation does not work. One may be tempted to start with a contract, but that runs the risk of setting the relation off on the foot of distrust, which is difficult to turn around. If one has the time, one may start with small investments and up the ante as trust grows. That may be too slow. An alternative is to call in the help of a trustworthy go-between.

The problem of dependence and negative power is especially acute if the relation requires 'specific investments', which are dedicated to the partner and lose value when the relationship breaks. Such investments arise to enhance quality and enable cooperation in the endeavour of Schumpeterian 'novel combinations' of innovation. This creates dependence that the partner may utilise to gain leverage in negotiation, with the threat of exiting from the relation, leaving the partner with a useless investment. A solution is to share the property, and with it the risk of the investment. Also, one needs to be confident that the relation will last sufficiently long to recoup the investment. This goes against the rhetoric of maximum flexibility, and instead goes for optimal flexibility. Relations should last sufficiently long to elicit specific investments, but not so long as to create rigidity.

Another question, at least as important but seldom asked, is how to end a relationship. One way is to prepare one's departure in secret, on the sly, no longer making specific investments, and taking the time to seek a new partner. The motive for doing this is not to give the partner time and opportunity to try and keep him from leaving. It is a well-known phenomenon in behavioural economics that people act more extremely when they stand to lose something of value, in a 'loss frame', than when they set out to gain something. It is known from social psychology and behavioural economics that people in such a frame of mind are prone to more extreme behaviour than when standing to gain in a relationship. People are known to try and tie down their partner in front of a judge while they do not stand a chance. The alternative is to timely announce one's departure, to let the partner make no more specific investments and allow for more preparation of exit, and promise to help find a new partner. The risk is that thereby one allows time for the partner to resist. But if the relation was one of give and take and trust, the approach of secret preparations of selfish exit would be unexpected, would not be seen as in good faith, and might evoke a vociferous response, damaging one's reputation.

There is a sociological theory of 'relational signalling'. It proposes that in relations one can be in different mental frames (Lindenberg 2003). A frame of thinking determines how one perceives and interprets observed actions, and how one responds to it. One frame is that of 'protecting one's resources'. It is self-interested, based on an instinct, developed in evolution, of survival. From that frame, one will scrutinise actions for evidence of threat, and is tempted to surrender to suspicion and 'exit' as opposed to 'voice' (Hirschman 1970). The second frame is that of 'solidarity', where one is prepared to trust and engage in informal give and take, and altruism, up to a point, from the instinct, also developed in evolution, of wanting to collaborate and engage in empathy and voice. There, when an expectation is unfulfilled, the default is to 'voice' this, with the intent of trying 'to sort things out' and trying to solve problems with mutual effort. When that fails one can fall back on exit. From one frame of thought it can be difficult to switch to the other frame: the frame one is in can be robust, especially the one of guarding resources. The solidarity frame is needed for trust. One will observe actions as evidence of the frame the other is in, and one will try to prevent the switch away from the solidarity frame. This is the notion of 'relational signalling'. Seemingly trivial actions may count, such as failing to respond to an e-mail, or treatment of a waiter in a restaurant.

All this is part of the dynamic capability of managing collaborative relations for innovation.

Digital Technologies

Digital technologies, such as the Internet, algorithms, machine learning and robots, yield many conveniences, such as search engines, e-mail, smartphones, route planners, social media and enhanced efficiency, but with mixed blessings, and disadvantages such as fake news, hate mail and vicious Twitter, breaches of privacy, echo chambers with people only communicating with like-minded. Social media were supposed to bring people together, but 'on any issue where there is incipient polarisation, machine learning can target a user with a news story or opinion slightly more extreme, thereby reinforcing the polarization' (Burbridge et al. 2020, 9). The effects are sometimes presented as inevitable, like a law of nature, but most of it derives from attunement to our own opinion or habit, in choices of sources of information, goals, goods, opinions and news.

People are afraid of missing out on things. On social media, they want to profile themselves as happy and successful, they tend to follow those who appear to be more successful than themselves. As a result of seeking such comparisons, one can feel inferior. Attention is scarce, so one strives to draw away attention from others with ever more concise and hence impoverished and easily absorbed content. Attention spans get shorter, and attention gets more superficial (Burbridge et al. 2020, 87).

People let themselves be guided by algorithms, assuming that they are effective because engineered by specialists. Government officials favour them as supposedly objective and unemotional, in contrast with erratic and confused individuals. But those algorithms embody views and perspectives of their creators that are hidden. Algorithms are good at optimisation, consistency, wide scope of variables taken into account, variety of experience of different people and no myopia of self-serving judgements. However, as discussed before, values are often incommensurable, cannot be subsumed in a single variable, and imply the need for different dimensions in the evaluation. That is what a democracy needs to deal with, and it requires debate between people, not effacing differences of view in calculation that appears to be objective but is selective.

Speed of choice increases, while its quality lapses behind. Prosperity has lifted people to higher levels in Maslow's hierarchy of needs, which involves more choices, often between values that are incommensurable, and brings a deluge of data, by which attention becomes more needed but also scarcer. This requires more time, not less. There is a need for slow choice, with more reflection.

People are being led and coached by what is framed in the technology. Rather than forming opinions in interaction with others, seeing them act and perhaps discussing with them, they follow the technology, often blindly. It was emphasised, in this book, how cooperation was needed in human evolution and led to a sense of reciprocity and even altruism that is now being eroded. They are not after a common good but at what they assume is in their personal interest. They do not reflect on the often tacit goals and ethics implicit in what they are enticed into. The technology is often presented as value-free and self-evident, but is based on a tacit ideology.

An obvious example is the regulation employed against the corona crisis, aimed at objective and tangible values of safety and health, based on 'objective' specialist assessment and ignoring less tangible and more subjective values of bodily contact, interpersonal interaction and social activity. The problem is that there are good reasons for them, but they erode intimacy and privacy, as, for example, with the telephone apps to trace and control contagion.

In augmented reality, virtual worlds are personalised, increasing distance between people, and generating inequality in the quality and cost of the means used (Burbridge et al. 2020, 46). Much is produced to increase ease and comfort, but Burbridge et al. claim 'that liberal democratic citizenship requires a certain amount of discomfort – enough to motivate citizens to pursue improvements' (46).

How did all this come about? I think that one fundamental cause of the focus on speed and efficiency is that digital technologies are shaped from what Rosa (2016, 2019) has explained as an orientation towards the hedonist value of life as pleasure: we try to cram as much consumption and entertainment as possible in limited life, and enhanced efficiency serves that, with ever faster and more satisfaction. Again: it does not just happen to us, but we implicitly call for it, and the technicians craft it for us.

A second cause lies in the dodging of ethical considerations of the good life, in daily life, and in business, as engendered by the liberal heritage of considering ethics as a private, not a public matter, and even a sign of totalitarianism, and not a task of government or business, offering an escape in mere 'compliance'.

There is benevolent, paternalistic manipulation in pushing people in directions of greatest self-interest that are not subjected to discussion, and taken for granted. Not only are preferences taken for granted, without discussion, but they are moulded to the convenience and purpose of firms and governments. A recent example is that of *nudging* (Sunstein and Thaler 2003). Social psychology has demonstrated that people are very imperfect in their decision-making, with routinely non-rational, non-optimal choice resulting from 'decision heuristics', inertia, 'framing', 'anchors' and lack of self-control, discussed elsewhere. This discovery has stimulated 'nudging', which aims to reduce these imperfections by pushing people towards choices that are better for themselves or third parties, or public interest. Even libertarians argue for 'libertarian paternalism', defined as nudging that is to the benefit of the subject itself (paternalist), while leaving open the choice to accept the nudge or not (libertarian). It is libertarian 'benevolence' if it is in the interest of third parties or the collective.

Nudging can take many forms. One example is the use of nudging to get people to adopt a healthier life style, in healthy food and more exercise, avoiding obesity. The idea is that people suffer from lack of self-control and lack of a long-term perspective, by which they harm themselves (paternalism) or create high collective costs of medical care (benevolence). The nudge might be a higher health insurance premium for unhealthy life styles (premium selection).

An important case is the question of 'opt-in' or 'opt-out'. For example, in organ donation, the 'default' may be that it is not permitted, unless one gives explicit permission, or, the other way around, one is assumed to give permission unless otherwise indicated. The latter yields more donation than the former, mostly as a result of inertia: one does not want to take the trouble of making an explicit decision and falls back on the default on offer. A contrasting possibility is to force people to make an explicit, conscious decision for or against donation, and then specify that (e.g. on one's driver's license).

Proponents of nudging claim that there is no alternative, but there is. It is to try and build explicit motivation of people by convincing and coaching them. Technology can be used to help make the goals of instruments and their tacit ethics explicit and facilitate discussion about them. Nudging circumvents that. Intrinsic motivation through ethical awareness is more humane, and is likely to be more stable and self-generating, and then also cheaper, more efficient, than subconscious manipulation.

Take the case of obesity, with the nudge of higher insurance premiums. Proponents of nudging claim that there is no alternative. But there is. For obesity the alternative is for doctors or counsellors to try and convince people to engage in a different life style, and to train and coach them in it. That could be promoted with insurance companies paying for it. When it succeeds, the effect is more durable than the material incentive of an insurance premium, which lasts only as long as it is maintained. People then don't act in a certain way because they are rewarded for it but because they think it is better.

More widely, the Internet can be used to mitigate negative effects of 'echo chambers', such as to build in incentives to online communities to take note of rival or complementary views, to build in a slowing down of choice and promote reflection, to build in more reflection on underlying values in the choice of products and sources of information, to signal fake news (as is already tried), to have online discussion with face-to-face views, as we have learned to do during the quarantine in the corona crisis.

Robots

There is talk of robots developing beyond human cognitive capacity. There is fear that they will even come to dominate humans. In particular, the fear is that they will behave like sociopaths, with superior rationality but without human morality, without human values of empathy, compassion and without practical wisdom of action. If there is any ground to this fear, should we bring in moral sense in the design and development of robots? How is that to be done? It requires, I propose, collaboration between engineers, software developers, cognitive and neural scientists, psychologists and philosophers.

But first, let us consider how robots could equal and surpass human cognition. That would require, among other things, a capability to develop tacit knowledge and associative, creative thought. Could that be part of machine learning? Earlier, I discussed how cognition might develop in the brain, in 'neural Darwinism'. I see no reason why that could not be emulated in robot brains. In fact, present robots already have been programmed to have an evolutionary learning capacity, where more or less random trials are reinforced or weakened in performance.

How about morality, then? I argued earlier that in humans moral instincts have evolved in a long process of evolution, with rival instincts of self-interest and altruism. For robotics to reproduce this, the development of robots, with some selection process in their functioning, would have to be speeded up enormously to match the long evolution of the human brain. Perhaps that can be done. But who defines and sets the selection conditions for survival of conduct? What if those are somehow set to *prevent* the selection of altruism, for the sake of efficiency perhaps?

Earlier, I argued that in human evolution an instinct for altruism might have developed from a benefit in group selection, under certain conditions, and that in-group loyalty probably arose, at the price of out-group discrimination. Would this also have to be reproduced in the evolution of robots? And couldn't humans then be seen as the out-group, suffering all the more from robots?

Alternatively, could robots be programmed to act morally according to the multiple causality of action discussed previously? They would then have to be made to adequately perceive situations in a morally relevant way (material cause), to interpret their moral import and match them to moral principles (formal cause), taking into account situational conditions (conditional cause), depending on the agent and its position and role (efficient cause).

Burbridge et al. (2020) noted that people die and machines do not. Kierkegaard proposed life as a process of making choices and acting on them in the face of certain future death at an uncertain date. Heidegger spoke of being unto death ('Sein zum Tode'). That shapes life and its decisions. Aristotle spoke of 'eudaimonia' as encompassing the whole of life. The value of something is to be seen in the context of the whole of limited life. Could that apply to robots?

Would robots also need to take into account their own interests such as their own survival or 'health', not to self-destruct too easily? And what moral principles would be programmed, according to what ethical system?

Utilitarianism, Kantian duty ethics or some form of virtue ethics? Would there be exemplary robots for robots to imitate (exemplary cause)? Or could they learn to imitate their human teachers? Or could humans at some point learn from exemplary robots?

In the exercise of practical wisdom intersubjective debate is needed, in *debatable ethics*, between different moral perspectives and assessments of situations, to fine-tune, moderate or revise moral perspectives. Would such debate need to occur between robots and humans, or robots among themselves? Or would robots help in debates between humans? To sharpen their moral sense and become morally more adept, would it help to let robots read literature? Could they produce literature for humans to sharpen their moral sense? What will happen when robots take on more and more tasks, with increasing intelligence? What if a robot is opinionated, its views going against the established order, or against the will of its maker or owner?

Presently, an intellectual, scientist or worker on a shop floor with contrary views cannot easily be silenced, in democracies. But robots may be simply switched off, or reprogrammed to conform. What will this do to people, if with regard to robots they no longer need to defend their views, and can bend the views of robots to their own? Would people then prefer to consort with robots, for the ease and comfort of it? Would that make them more self-involved, narcissistic even, turning robots into mirrors?

I have argued that one needs the opposition from the other to detect one's own myopia, to nourish a flourishing life. This is needed, I argued, to achieve the highest form of freedom, which includes freedom from the bias of the self. If robots are self-learning, by adapting their intelligence to what is successful, more rigorously and perfectly than humans, will this be a source of contrariness, defiance? People have a variety of sources of experience, in jobs, families, friendship, sports, travel and chance encounters, to feed their cognition and morality. Will robots have access to such diversity of experience? Will the owner of the robot, having invested in it, be willing to grant it unproductive time, in a range of private activities?

Next to his notions of 'exit' and 'voice', Albert Hirschman recognised the possibility of 'loyalty', which is acceptance, surrender to a suppressive relationship. It is submissive but is often given an intrinsic value by ritualisation, as insertion in an order in which one may even feel at home. Robots may undergo forced exit, being switched off, or may be programmed for loyalty. Will they be allowed to raise voice, or even be programmed for it? Or will they ever be self-generative enough to grasp voice, or even to impose loyalty?

I have long (since the 1980s) been a proponent of a universal basic income (UBI). I will not here go into the arguments for and against, the potential and the risks that robots will replace human employment. In the past, technology destroyed existing employment but also created new, giving a net increase. However, that went along with a shortening of labour hours and an increase in part-time labour. In the present technological revolution the effect may be different, because the innovation is multilevel, by which I mean that robots are not only applied to existing jobs but also for producing robots that produce robots that produce robots, while earlier technologies did not have that feature. Light bulbs did not produce light bulbs. Opinions are divided on this issue, but one might impose a tax on the use of robots for services, such as care and company for the elderly, drivers, delivery, automated cars and so on, and use that as a contribution to the financing of a UBI. A drawback of tax on capital is that it may drive away business to another country, but here that does not apply since the tax is on use in the domestic economy, which cannot flee.

CONCLUSIONS

Everything moves, as the ancient Greek philosopher Heraclitus said. Underlying processes are evolution, with the principles of mutation, gene expression, selection and transmission, and the force of increasing entropy. Life is a fight against this force.

A physical object is a constellation of molecules, consisting of atoms and their constituents, partly as waves. An organism is a constellation of organs, fluids and neurons that interact in metabolism to produce a whole, whose identity evolves in interaction with its environment. Knowledge and theory develop in a cycle of assimilation and accommodation. Truth is warranted assertability, with arguments based on theory, facts, origins and utility, which may shift. Morality is based on virtues, whose selection and enactment depend on the conditions of action, with the supreme virtue of phronesis. Trust is a process, with varying conditions that affect trustworthiness, and requires phronesis. An organisation develops with shifts in its organisational focus as conditions change. A society is an uneasy, shifting balance between self-interest and community, guided and misled by ideologies and institutions, which may be sidetracked on a dead-end path with no return.

This book forms the basis for a range of books that elaborate on the different processes of things, identity, knowledge, morality and society.

REFERENCES

Abelson, R. P. 1976, 'Script processing in attitude formation and decision making', in J. S. Carroll and J. W. Payne (eds), *Cognition and social behavior*, New York: Taylor & Francis.
Aldrich, H. 1999, *Organizations evolving*, London: Sage.
Anderson, P., and M. Tushman. 1990, 'Technological, discontinuities and dominant designs: A cyclical model of technological change', Administrative Science Quarterly, 35/4, 604–33.
Baum, J. A. C., and J. V. Singh. 1994, 'Organizational hierarchies and evolutionary processes: Some reflections on a theory of organizational evolution', in J. A. C. Baum and J. V. Singh (eds), *Evolutionary dynamics of organizations*, Oxford: Oxford University Press, 3–20.
Aristotle. 1999, *Ethica Nicomachea*, Dutch translation, Groningen: Historische Uitgeverij.
Bachelard, G. 1950, *La dialectique de la durée*, Paris: Presses Universitaires de France.
Bergson, Henri. 1900, *Le rire: Essay sur la signification du comique*, Paris: Presses Universitaires de France.
———. 1969, *L'évolution creatrice*, Paris: Presses Universitaires de France.
Bourdieu, Pierre. 2018, *Outline of a theory of practice*, Cambridge: Cambridge University Press.
Boyd, R., and P. J. Richerson. 1985, *Culture and the evolutionary process*, Chicago: University of Chicago Press.
Brown, J. S., and P. Duguid 1996, 'Organizational learning and communities of practice', in M. D. Cohen and L. S. Sproull (eds), *Organizational learning*, London: Sage, 58–82.
Bruni, Luigino, and Robert Sugden. 2008, 'Fraternity: Why the market need not be a morally free zone', *Economics and Philosophy*, 24/1, 35–64.
———. 2013, 'Reclaiming virtue ethics for economics', *Journal of Economic Perspectives*, 27/1, 141–64.
Burbridge, Daniel, Andrew Biggs and Michael Reiss. 2020, *Citizenship in a networked age: An agenda for rebuilding our civic ideals*, funded by Templeton World Charity Foundation, Oxford: Oxford University Press.
British Home Office. 1999, *Restorative justice: An overview*, London: British Home Office.
Buonomano, Dean. 2017, *Your brain is a time machine*, New York: W.W. Norton.
Burgelman, R. A. 1983, 'A model of the interaction of strategic behavior, corporate context, and the concept of strategy', *Academy of Management Review*, 8, 61–70.
Capra, Fritjof. 1975, *The Tao of physics: An exploration of the parallels between modern physics and eastern mysticism*, London: Wildwood House.
Campbell, D. T. 1974, 'Evolutionary epistemology', in P. A. Schilpp (ed.), *The philosopphy of Karl R. Popper*, Lasalle, IL: Open Court, 412–63.

Campbell, D. T. 1987, 'Blind variation and selective retention as in other knowledge processes', reprinted in 1988, 'Evolutionary epistemology', in D. T. Campbell, *Methodology and epistemology for social science*, Oxford: Oxford University Press, 393–434.

Chesbrough, H. 2003, *Open innovation: The new imperative for creating and profiting from technology*, Boston: Harvard Business School Press.

Cohen, M. D., and D. A. Levinthal. 1990, 'Absorptive capacity: A new perspective on learning innovation', *Administrative Science Quarterly*, 35, 128–52.

Copleston, Frederick, 1964–67, *A history of philosophy*, vols. 1–8, London: Image Books.

Craver, Carl F. 2007, *Explaining the brain*, Oxford: Oxford University Press.

Daly, Kathleen. 2001, *Restorative justice: The true story*, paper presented to the Scottish Criminality Conference.

Damasio, Antonio R. 2003, *Looking for Spinoza*, Orlando, FL: Harcourt.

Danneels, E. 2003, 'Tight–loose coupling with customers: The enactment of customer orientation', *Strategic Management Journal*, 24/6, 559–76.

Dawkins, R. 1983, 'Universal darwinism', in D. S. Bendall (ed.), *Evolution from molecules to man*, Cambridge: Cambridge University Press, 403–25.

De Dreu, Carsten, Daniel Balliet and Nir Halevy. 2014, 'Parochial cooperation in humans: Forms and functions of self-sacrifice in intergroup conflict', *Advances in Motivation Science*, 1, 1–47.

DeLanda, Manuel. 2016, *Assemblage theory*, Edinburgh: Edinburgh University Press.

Deleuze, Gilles, and Felix Guattari. 1991, *Qu'est ce que la philosophie?* Paris: Les Editions de Minuit.

de Saussure, Ferdinand. 1979, *Course de linguistique générale*, Payotèque, Paris: Payot.

Dethier, Hubert. 1993, *Het gezicht en het raadsel*, Brussels: VUB Press.

De Wit, Bob, and Ron Meyer. 2017, *Strategy: An international perspective*, Andover, UK: Cengage Learning EMEA.

Dobyns, Stephen. 2011, Next word better word. The craft of writing poetry, London: Palgrave MacMillan.

Dosi, G., R. R. Nelson and S. Winter. 2000, *The nature and dynamics of organizational capabilities*, Oxford: Oxford University Press.

Edelman, Gerald M. 1987, *Neural Darwinism: The theory of neuronal group selection*, New York: Basic Books.

Eldredge, N., and S. J. Gould. 1972, 'Punctuated equilibria: An alternative to phyletic gradualism', in T. J. M. Schopf (ed.), *Models in paleobiology*, San Franciso, CA: Freeman, Cooper, 82–115.

Flavell, J. H. 1967, *The developmental psychology of Jean Piaget*, Princeton, NJ: Van Nostrand.

Foster, J., and J. S. Metcalfe (eds). 2001, *Frontiers of evolutionary economics: Competition, self-organization and innovation policy*, Cheltenham, UK: Edward Elgar.

Fukuyama, Francis. 1995, *Trust: The social virtues and the creation of prosperity*, New York: Free Press.

———. 2018, *Identity*, London: Profile Books.

Fry, Stephen. 2005, The ode less travelled, London: Arrow Books.

Gadamer, Hans-George. 1975, 'Hermeneutics and social science', *Cultural Hermeneutics*, 2/4, 307–16.

Garud, R., and M. A. Rappa. 1996, 'A socio-cognitive model of technology evolution; The case of cochlear implants', in J. R. Meindl, C. Stubbart and J. F. Porac (eds), *Cognition within and between organisations*, London: Sage, 441–74; first published in 1994 in *Organization Science*, 5(3).

Garcia, Tristan. 2014, *Form and object*, Edinburgh: Edinburgh University Press.
Gersick, C. J. G. 1988, 'Time and transition in work teams: Toward a new model of group development', *Academy of Management Journal*, 31, 9–41.
Gould, S. J. 1989, 'Punctuated equilibrium in fact and theory', *Journal of Social Biological Structure*, 12, 117–36.
Groot, A. D. de. 1969, *Methodology: Foundations of inference and research in the social sciences*, The Hague: Mouton.
Hannan, M. T., and J. Freeman. 1977, 'The population ecology of organizations', *American Journal of Sociology*, 88, 929–64.
———. 1984, 'Structural inertia and organizational change', *American Sociological Review*, 49, 149–64.
———. 1989, *Organizational ecology*, Cambridge, MA: Harvard University Press.
Harman, Graham. 2018, *Object-oriented ontology*, n.p.: Penguin.
Henderson, R. M., and K. Clark. 1990, 'Architectural innovation: The reconfiguration of existing product technologies and the failure of established firms', *Administrative Science Quarterly*, 35, 9–30.
Hintikka, Jaakko. 1975 *The intentions of intentionality and other new models for modalities*, Dordrecht, Holland: Reidel.
Hayek, Friedrich von. 1945, 'The use of knowledge in society', *American Economic Review*, 35/4, 519–30.
Hirschman, A. O. 1970, *Exit, voice and loyalty*, Cambridge, MA: Harvard University Press.
Hodgson, Geoffrey. 1998, 'The approach of institutional economics', *Journal of Economic Literature*, 36, 166–92.
———. 2002a, 'The legal nature of the firm and the myth of the firm-market hybrid', *International Journal of the Economics of Business*, 9/1, 37–60.
———. 2002b, 'Darwinism in economics: From analogy to ontology', *Journal of Evolutionary Economics*, 12, 259–81.
———. 2006, 'What are institutions?', *Journal of Economic Issues*, 60/1, 1–25.
———. 2019, *Is there a future for heterodox economics?*, Cheltenham UK: Edward Elgar.
Hodgson, G. M., and T. Knudsen. 2004, 'The firm as interactor', *Journal of Evolutionary Economics*, 14, 281–307.
———. 2006, 'Why we need a generalized Darwinism, and why generalized Darwinism is not enough', *Journal of Economic Behavior and Organization*, 61, 1–19.
Holland, John. H. [1975] 1992, *Adaptation in natural and artificial systems*, Boston: MIT Press.
———. [1995] 1996, *Hidden order: How adaptation builds complexity*, Cambridge: Perseus Books.
Hull, D. L. 1988, *Science as process: An evolutionary account of the social and conceptual development of science*, Chicago: University of Chicago Press.
Inglehart, Ronald, and Christian Welzel. 2014, *Modernization, cultural change and democracy: The human development sequence*, Cambridge: Cambridge University Press.
Janow, Richard. 2003, 'Shannon entropy applied to productivity of organisations', published in *IEMC '03 Proceedings, Managing technologically driven organizations: The human side of innovation and change*, 2–4 November 2003, Albany, NY: *IEEE Xplore*.
Johnson-Laird, P. N. 1983, *Mental models*, Cambridge: Cambridge University Press.
Johnston, A. 2008, *Zizek's ontology: A transcendental materialist theory of subjectivity*, Evanston, IL: North Western University Press.
Kirzner, I. 1973, *Competition and entrepreneurship*. Chicago: University of Chicago Press.
Klein Woolthuis, Rosalinde, B. Hillebrand and B. Nooteboom. 2005, 'Trust, contract and relationship development', *Organization Studies*, 26/, 813–40.

REFERENCES

Knight, F. H. 1921, *Risk, uncertainty, and profit*, New York: Houghton Mifflin.
Kogut, B., and U. Zander. 1996, 'What firms do? Coordination, identity, and learning', *Organization Science*, 7/5, 502–16.
Kuhn, Tomas. 1970 (2nd edition), *The structure of scientific revolutions*, London: University of Chicago Press.
Lachmann, L. M. 1956, Capital and its structure, London: Bell.
———. 1978, 'An Austrian stocktaking: Unsettled questions and tentative answers', in L. Spadaro (ed.), *New directions in Austrian economics*, Kansas City, MO: Sheed, Andrews & McMeel, 1–18.
Lakatos, Imre. 1978, *The methodology of scientific research programmes*, Cambridge: Cambridge University Press.
Lakatos, Imre, and Alan Musgrave. 1970, *Criticism and the growth of knowledge*, Cambridge: Cambridge University Press.
Lakoff, G., and M. Johnson. 1999, *Philosophy in the* Flesh, New York: Basis Books.
Leman, Patrick, Andy Bremmer, Ross D. Parker and Mary Gauvain. 2019, *Developmental psychology*, New York: McGraw-Hill.
Liisberg, Sune, Esther Oluffa Pedersen and Anne Line Dalsgard. 2015, *Anthropology and philosophy: Dialogues on trust and hope*, Oxford: Berghahn Books.
Lindenberg, S. 2003, 'Governance seen from a framing point of view: The employment relationship and relational signalling', in Bart Nooteboom and Frédérique E. Six (eds), *The trust process: Empirical studies of the determinants and the process of trust development*, Cheltenham, UK: Edward Elgar, 37–57.
Maalouf, Amin. 2019, *Le naufrage des civilisations*, Paris: Grasset.
MacIntyre, Alistair. 2011, *After virtue*, London: Bloomsbury.
March, James G. 1991, 'Exploration and exploitation in organizational learning', *Organization Science*, 2/1, 101–23.
McKelvey, W. 1982, *Organizational systematics: Taxonomy, evolution, classification*, Berkeley: University of California Press.
Malachowski, Alan. 2013, *The Cambridge companion to pragmatism*, Cambridge: Cambridge University Press.
Marmysz, John. 2003, *Laughing at nothing: Humor as a response to nihilism*, Albany: State University of New York Press.
Mead, George H. 2011, *G.H. Mead: A reader*, Filipe Carreira da Silva (ed.), New York: Routledge.
Merleau-Ponty, Maurice. 1974, *Phenomenology, language and sociology*, London: Heinemann.
Metcalfe, J. S. 1998, *Evolutionary economics and creative destruction*, London: Routledge.
Metzinger, Thomas. 2009, *The ego tunnel: The science of the mind and the myth of the self*, New York: Basic Books.
Milbank, John, and Adrian Pabst. 2016, *The politics of virtue: Post liberalism and the human future*, London: Rowman & Littlefield.
Miner, A. S. 1991, 'Organizational evolution and the social ecology of jobs', *American Sociological Review*, 56, 772–85.
Mokyr, J. 1990, *The lever of riches: Technological creativity and economic progress*, Oxford: Oxford University Press.
Moellering, Guido. 2009, 'Leaps and Lapses of Faith: Exploring the Relationship Between Trust and Deception', in B. Herrington (ed.) *Deception: From Ancient Empires to Internet Dating*, Stanford, CA: Stanford University Press, 137–53.
Moseley, Roger. 2019, *Morality: A natural history*, Victoria, BC: Friesen Press.

Narayaman, V. K., L. J. Lee and B. Kamerer. 2011, 'The cognitive perspective in strategy: An integrative review', *Journal of Management*, 37/11, 305–51.
Nelson, Julie A. 2009. 'A response to Bruni and Sugden', *Economics and Philosophy*, 25, 187–93.
Nelson, Richard R. 2008, 'Economic development from the perspective of evolutionary economic theory', *Oxford Development Studies*, 36/1, 9–21.
Nelson, R. R., and Sidney Winter. 1982, *An evolutionary theory of economic change*, Cambridge: Cambridge University Press.
Nicholson, Carol. 2013, 'Education and the pragmatic temperament', in Malachowski (ed.), *The Oxford companion to Pragmatism*, Cambridge: Cambridge University Press, 249–72.
Nietzsche, Friedrich. [1887] 2013, *On the genealogy of morals: A polemic*, n.p.: Penguin Classics
Nonaka, I., and H. Takeuchi. 1995, *The knowledge creating company*, Oxford: Oxford University Press.
Nooteboom, Bart. 1992, 'Towards a dynamic theory of transactions', *Journal of Evolutionary Economics*, 2, 281–99.
———. 1999, *Inter-firm alliances: Analysis and design*, London: Routledge.
———. 2000, *Learning and innovation in organisations and economies*, Oxford: Oxford University Press.
———. 2001, 'From evolution to language and learning', in J. Foster and S. Metcalfe (eds), *Frontiers of evolutionary economics: Competition, self-organisation and innovation policy*, Cheltenham, UK: Edward Elgar, 41–69.
———. 2002, *Trust: Forms, foundations, functions, failures and figures*, Cheltenham UK: Edward Elgar.
———. 2006, 'Elements of cognitive theory of the firm', in E. Krecké, C. Krecké, R. G. Koppl (eds), *Cognition and economics*, Advances in Austrian Economics, vol. 9, Amsterdam, Elsevier, 145–76.
———. 2009, *A cognitive theory of the firm: Learning, governance and dynamic capabilities*, Cheltenham, UK: Edward Elgar.
———. 2012, *Beyond Humanism: The flourishing of life, self and other*, London: Palgrave MacMillan.
———. 2019a, *Uprooting economics: A manifesto for change*, Cheltenham, UK: Edward Elgar.
———. 2019b, 'Uncertainty and the economic need for trust', in M. Sasaki (ed.) *Trust in contemporary society*, Leiden, Netherlands: Brill.
Nooteboom, Bart, Wim P. M. Van Haverbeke, Geert M. Duysters, Victor A. Gilsing and Ad van den Oord. 2007, 'Optimal cognitive distance and absorptive capacity', *Research Policy*, 36, 1016–34.
North, Douglas. 1990, The limits of rationality. University of Chicago Press.
Okrent, Mark. 2013, 'Heidegger's pragmatism redux', in Malachowski (ed.), *The Oxford companion to Pragmatism*, Cambridge: Cambridge University Press, 124–59.
Orr, J. 1996, *Talking about machines: An ethnography of a modern job*, Ithaca, NY: ILR Press, Cornell University.
Piaget, Jean. 1970, *Psychologie et epistémologie*, Paris: Denoël.
———. 1974, *Introduction a l'épistémologie génétique*, Paris: Presses Universitaires de France.
Popper, Karl R. 1959, *The logic of scientific discovery*, London: Hutchison.
Radnitzky, Gerard, and W. W. Bartley III (eds). 1987, *Evolutionary epistemology, rationality, and the sociology of knowledge*, La Salle, IL: Open Court, 91–114.
Romanelli, E., and M. Y. Tushman. 1994, 'Organizational transformation as punctuated equilibrium: An empirical test', *Academy of Management Journal*, 37/5, 1141–66.

Rosa, Hartmut. 2016, *Leven in tijden van versnelling*, Amsterdam: Boom.
———. 2019, *Resonance: A sociology of our relationship to the world*, Cambridge: Polity Press.
Rosenberg, Alexander. 2000, *Darwinism in philosophy, social science and policy*, Cambridge: Cambridge University Press.
Rosch, Eleanor. 1978, 'Principles of categorization', in Eleanor Rosch and B. B. Lloyd (eds), *Cognition and categorization*, Hillsdake, MI: Erlbaum.
Rovelli, Carlo. 2016, *Reality is not what it seems*, n.p.: Penguin.
Schein, Edgar H. 1985, *Organizational culture and leadership*, San Francisco, CA: Jossey Bass.
Shackle, G. 1961, *Decision, order and time in human affairs*, Cambridge: Cambridge University Press.
Sherman, Lawrence W., and Heather Strang. 2007, *Restorative justice: The evidence*, London: Esmée Fairbairn Foundation.
Schank, R., and R. Abelson. 1977, *Scripts, plans, goals and understanding: An inquiry into human knowledge structures*, Hillsdale, NJ: Erlbaum.
Smircich, L. 1983, 'Organization as shared meaning', in L. R. Pondy, P. J. Frost, G. Morgan and T. C. Dandridge (eds), *Organizational symbolism*, Greenwich, CT: JAI Press, 55–65.
Smith, Peter B., and Michael Harris Bond. 1993, *Social psychology across cultures*, London: Prentice Hall.
Spender, J. C. 1983, *Industry recipes*, Oxford: Basil Blackwell.
Stroud, B. 1977, *Hume*, The Arguments of Philosophers, London: Routledge and Kegan Paul.
Sunstein, Cass R., and Richard H. Thaler. 2003, 'Libertarian paternalism is not an oxymoron', *University of Chicago Law Review*, 70/4, 1159–202.
Teece, D. 2007, 'Explicating dynamic capabilities: The nature and microfoundations of (sustainable) enterprise performance', *Strategic Management Journal*, 28, 1319–50.
Teece, D., G. Pisano and A. Shuen. 1997, 'Dynamic capabilities and strategic management', in G. Dosi, R. R. Nelson and S. Winter (eds), *The nature and dynamics of organizational capabilities*, Oxford: Oxford University Press.
Testa, Bernard, and Lemont B. Kier. 2000, 'Emergence and dissolvence in the self-organization of complex systems', *Entropy*, 2, 1–25.
Theil, Henri. 1967, *Economics and information theory*, Chicago: Rand McNally.
Thiel, Christian. 1965, *Sinn und Bedeutung in der Logik Gottlob Frege's*, Meisenheimam Glan: Anton Hain.
Tomasello, Michael. 2016, *A natural history of human morality*, Cambridge, MA: Harvard University Press.
Tsoukas, Haridimos, and Robert Chia. 2002, 'On organizational becoming: Rethinking organisational change', *Organization Science*, 13/5, 567–82.
Tushman, M. L., and E. Romanelli. 1985, 'Organizational evolution: A metamorphosis model of convergence and reorientation', in B. A. Staw and L. L. Cummings(eds), *Research in organizational behavior*, Greenwich, CT: JAI Press, 171–222.
Tushman, M. L., and P. Anderson. 1986, 'Technological discontinuities and organizational environments', *Administrative Science Quarterly*, 31, 439–65.
Veblen, T. 2009, The theory of the leisure class; An economic study of institutions, Portland, OR: Floating Press.
Weick, Karl F. 1995, *Sensemaking in organisations*, Thousand Oaks, CA: Sage.
Weick, Karl F., and K. H. Roberts. 1993, 'Collective mind in organizations', *Administrative Science Quarterly*, 39, reprinted in Michael D. Cohen and L. S. Sproull (eds), *Organizational learning*, 1996, London: Sage, 330–58.

Wilhelm, Richard. 2003, *I ching or book of changes*, n.p.: Penguin.
Williamson, Oliver E. 1993, 'Calculativeness, Trust and Economic Organization', *Journal of Law and Economics*, 36, 453–86.
Witt, Ulrich. 2004, 'On the proper interpretation of "evolution" in economics and its implications for production theory', *Journal of Economic Methodology*, 11, 125–46.
———. 2005, 'The evolutionary perspective on organizational change and the theory of the firm', in K. Dopfer (ed.), *The evolutionary foundations of economics*, Cambridge: Cambridge University Press, 339–64.
Wittgenstein, Ludwig. [1953] 1976, *Philosophical investigations*, Oxford: Basil Blackwell.
Yamagishi, T., and M. Yamagishi. 1994, 'Trust and Commitment in the United States and Japan', *Motivation and Emotion*, 18, 129–66.
Woo, Henry K. H. 1992, *Cognition, value and price, a general theory of value*, Ann Arbor: University of Michigan Press.
Zollo, M., and S. G. Winter. 2002, 'Deliberate learning and the evolution of dynamic capabilities', *Organization Science*, 13/3, 339–51.

INDEX

absorptive capacity 25, 33, 38, 40, 46, 50, 77
accommodation 9, 45, 46, 48, 49
adaptation 1, 4, 12, 41, 45
affirmation 11, 12
agent-based simulation 49
Aldrich, H. 24, 26
algorithms 106
allopatric speciation 47
ambiguity 54, 70
analytic truth 51
apprenticeship 25
Aristotle 5, 8, 12, 43, 71, 80, 92, 94, 95, 96, 109
art 9
assimilation 46, 50
assumptions 3, 11, 29, 52, 89
    fundamental assumptions 39
    subsidiary/background assumptions 29, 30, 50
augmented reality 107
authenticity 35, 68–70, 88
authoritarian regimes 68, 75

Bachelard, Gaston 7, 10–11, 70–71
background assumptions 29, 30, 50
Bacon, Francis 71
Bandura, Albert 12
behavioural economics 43, 104–5
behavioural science, and evolution 16
belief 54
Bentham, Jeremy 92, 94
Bergson, Henri 6, 10, 13, 56, 64, 65, 69, 71, 97
Bergsonian flow of time 12
biological evolution 17, 18, 27

biology
    co-evolution 18
    interactors and replicators in 20
Bourdieu, Pierre 72, 77
brain 31, 32
Bruni, Luigino 99, 101, 102
Buddhism 3
Burbridge, Daniel 107, 109

Campbell, D. T. 27, 48, 51
Capra, Fritjof 3
categorical imperative 94
causality 4–5, 16, 73
causality of action 70–71
causality types 70, 97
causation 4, 5, 7, 55, 58–59, 60, 70
change 12–13
Chia, Robert 6, 39
civilisation 73
Climacus, Johannes 11, 13, 49–50, 69, 109
co-evolution 18–19, 23, 24
cognition 32–33, 44
cognitive distances 32–33, 38, 40, 63, 77
cognitive leadership 39
collaboration, and variation 50–51
collective identity 76, 77, 83
communication 40, 50, 53
communities 79, 83–85
comparative advantage 79
competition 13, 16–17, 18–19, 23, 25, 32, 36, 95, 98
complementarity 2, 3, 34, 62–63
complex adaptive systems (CAS) 19, 26, 34, 59, 69, 76
computer simulation 23, 49
conatus 11, 97

conduct, universality of 73–74
connectedness 1, 3, 36
consciousness 56
conservative revolution 36, 99
consolidation 45, 47, 49
conspiracies 98
constructivism 31–33
container metaphor 64, 76, 79, 93
contracts 82, 101
cooperation 95
Copenhagen interpretation of
 complementarity 62
corona crisis 4, 26, 36–37, 75, 98, 99, 106
courage 12, 94–95
creation 11, 12
creative destruction 39
credal identity 83
criminal justice 84
criticism 11, 12
cultural identity 67, 73–76
cultures 73
 of arbitrary group 76
 as complex adaptive system 76
 convergence of 75
 differences between 96
cycle of discovery 44, 46, 47, 48–49

Daly, Kathleen 85
Damasio, Antonio R. 31
de Saussure, Ferdinand 11, 55, 57,
 58, 69
debate 11
deconstruction 58
DeLanda, Manuel 7
Deleuze, Giles 6, 8, 12
Deleuze, Gilles 11
deliberate learning 44
Derrida, Jacques 7, 12, 58, 80
Dethier, Hubert 2
Dewey, John 4, 51, 90
différance 80
differentiation 45, 49
digital technologies 105–8
Dionysian vitalism 11
diversity 11, 16, 48, 93
DNA 6, 7, 19
dualism 31

duration 10–11
Durkheim, Émile 81
duty ethics 94, 110
dynamic capabilities 13, 43–44, 48,
 78, 82, 95

economic virtues 97–100
economics 12–13, 18
 evolutionary theory in 16
economies, and co-evolution 18
Edelman, Gerald 32, 68
Einstein, Albert 62
Eldredge, N. 47
elites 71–3
embodied cognition 20, 31
entelechy 12, 43
entropy 33–35, 36, 45, 46
 and knowledge 48
 and organisations 39–40
 of script 59
environment, damage to 1
environmental uncertainty 49
essence 5–6
eternal return 12
ethics 95
 and institutions 87–90
 Kantian ethics 94
 and purpose of life 90
eudaimonia 95, 109
evenness 34, 36, 39
evidence 5
evolution 8, 11, 15, 19, 47, 64, 91, 102
 and cooperation 95
 ecological side of 17–18
 genealogical side of 18
 interactors 19–22
 replicators 19–22
 and science 41–42
 selection 22–25
 universal Darwinism 16–19
 variation 25–27
 variety generation 15
experience 10
exploitation and exploration,
 distinguished 47
external goods 91
externality 1

INDEX

facial expressions 53, 74
fact and value, distinction between 30–31
failure 9
fake news 37, 105
falsification 9, 23, 29–30, 42
Feuerbach, Ludwig 88
Fichte, Johann Gottlieb 7
Figure 1. Design of the book 9
Flavell, J. H. 44
focus, mechanism and implementation of 40–41
Foster, J. 26
France 36
fraternity 99, 101, 102
free will 31, 56
freedom, negative and positive 35, 68
Frege, Gottlob 54, 55
French Revolution 68
friendship 73, 89, 101–2
Fukuyama, Francis 67, 83, 103

Gadamer, George 61
Garud, R. 23
gender roles 74
general concept 5–6
general will 68
generalisation 6, 42, 45, 46, 48
gestures 4, 53
globalisation 48, 75, 80
good life 67, 90, 96, 97
Gould, S. J. 47
Guattari, Felix 8

hawk and dove game 93
Hayek, Friedrich von 13, 16, 32–33, 98
Hegel, Georg Wilhelm Friedrich 7, 9, 11, 43
Heidegger, Martin 11, 68, 69, 95, 109
hermeneutic circle 61–62, 63
hierarchy 82–83
Hirschman, Albert 110
Hobbes, Thomas 88
Hodgson, Geoffrey 17, 20, 26–27, 87
Honneth, Axel 81
Hume, David 30, 32, 67, 71, 90, 91
humour 65–66, 69

Hutcheson, Francis 90
hybridisation 45, 47, 49

'I Ching' 3
ideas, association between 32
identity 4, 7, 67–68
    identity politics 36
    and networks (*See* networks)
ideologies 50
illusions 31
individual identity 67–68, 69
industry recipes 41
Inglehart, Ronald 74–75
inhibition 5
innovation 38, 59, 78
    and internationalisation 46
innovative potential 40
institutions, and ethics 87–90
intentional context 54
intentionality 1
interactionism 11, 31
interactors 17–18, 19–22, 23, 27, 42
internal goods 91, 95, 97
internationalisation 46
Internet 76, 108
invention, theory of 30
Iranian revolution 36

Johnston, A. 7
justice 64, 72, 84, 88, 89–90, 94, 95–96

Kant, Immanuel 51, 53, 94
Kantian problem 30
Kierkegaard. *See* Climacus, Johannes
Kirzner, I. 43
knowledge 25, 37–38, 97
    development of 43–49
    entropy 37–38
    and entropy 48
    from limits and failures 43
Knudsen, T. 17, 20, 26–27
Kuhn, Tomas 42

Lachmann, L. M. 38, 59
Lakatos, Imre 30
Lamarck, Jean-Baptiste 15
Lamarckian evolution 18, 20

language(s) 9, 32, 51, 53
  complementarity in 62–63
  differences between 61
  hermeneutic circle 61–62
  and langue 57–60
  and networks 78
  object bias 63–7
  and parole 57–60, 70
  and reference 54–57
  and sense 54–57, 70
  speech and writing 57–58
langue 57–60, 63, 69
learning 8
Levi Strauss, Claude 60
liberalism 35, 88
lobbying 98
loyalties 97, 109, 110
Lukacs, Georg 81
lying 6, 31, 44, 91, 94

Maalouf, Amin 35, 36, 98–99
Machiavelli, Niccolò 91
MacIntyre, Alistair 91
management, evolutionary theory in 16
Mandela, Nelson 35
Mandeville, Bernard de 89, 97
March, James G. 47
Maslow's hierarchy of needs 106
McKelvey, W. 21
Mead, G. H. 4, 53
meaning 58
memory 58
Merleau-Ponty, Maurice 31
metaphors 46, 57, 61–62, 64
Metcalfe, J. S. 26
metonymy 61–62
Metzinger, Thomas 56
Mill, John Stuart 92
modal context 54
models, compared with representations 32
moderation 94, 95
modern physics 2–3, 51, 64
monism 31
monopolies 36, 98, 99
moral sense 90, 96, 109, 110
morality 88–89, 90, 91, 97, 109
movement 10

multiple causality of action 5, 70, 71, 73, 109
multiple-channel rival system 23–24
mysticism 3

Narayaman, V. K. 43
national identity 77
nationalism 75, 79
negative freedom 35, 68, 69
Nelson, Julie A. 102
Nelson, Richard 17, 20, 21, 23, 26, 27, 87
networks 77–80, 83
neural Darwinism 32, 68
new knowledge, production of 37–38, 39
Nietzsche, Friedrich 11, 89, 97
Nietzschean drive to power 11–12
nodes 8, 58–60, 61, 83
nominalism 6
Nooteboom, Bart 47
North, Douglas 87
novel combinations 33, 38, 39–40, 42, 43, 48, 78, 104
nudging 107–8

object bias, in language 63–66
objective truth 4
object-oriented ontology 7
objects
  as events 10
  tendency and capacity of 7
Oger 12
oligopoly 36, 98
O'Neill, Joseph 54
optimal cognitive distance 33, 38, 47
organisational focus 21, 38–41
organisational identities 22, 39
organisational memory 43, 45
organisations 21, 38–41, 87
  culture 76
  entropy 39–40
  evolutionary theory of 19
  stabilisation of change 39
organizational 'cognitive focus' 39
other-interest 91

Parmenides 12
parochial altruism 93

parole 11, 55, 57–60, 61, 63, 69–70
Peirce, Charles Sanders 1
personal identity 67, 69, 76, 77
phenomena 3, 5, 10
philosophical orientation 1–7
philosophy 1–2
Piaget, Jean 9, 44
platform companies 98, 99
Plato 5, 11, 12, 96
poetry 57, 61–62
politics 35–37
    and co-evolution 18–19
Popper, Karl 9, 30, 42
populations 17
populism 71–72, 79, 83
positive freedom 35, 68, 69
positivism 29
postmodern philosophy 3
potentialisation 43
power, and relations 81
practical life 1
pragmatism 1, 4, 5
pre-practice testing 23
prewiring of the brain 92, 96
process philosophy 10–13
prototypes 6, 62
prudence 94
punctuated equilibria 47
purpose of life 90
puzzles 2

radical innovation 21, 25–26
Rappa, M. A. 23
reality 4, 8, 31, 53
reason 21, 31, 75, 94, 95, 96
reciprocation 45, 46–47, 48, 49
reciprocity 80, 88, 101, 106
recognition 81
reference 53, 54–57
relational signalling 105
relations 80–83, 102
relativity theory 29, 62
reliance 74, 94, 100–105
replication 25
replication and variety generation, relation between 25
replicators 17–18, 19–22, 42

representations 4, 31–32
reputation 5, 42, 67, 78, 82, 90, 92, 101, 103, 104
resonance 81, 99, 100
restaurant, nodes of 59–60
restorative justice 84–85
risk and uncertainty, difference between 49
rival methods 23–24
robots 108–11
Rorty, Richard 68
Rosa, Harmut 82
Rosa, Hartmut 80, 99, 107
Rosa, Helmut 100
Rousseau, Jean Jacques 67

sameness
    of meaning 54
    of reference 54
    of sense 54
Sartre, Jean-Paul 81
scanning 43–44
scenarios analysis 27
Schelling, Friedrich Wilhelm Joseph 43
Schumpeter, Joseph 42
science 41–43
    interactors and replicators in 18
    philosophy of 29–31
    replicators in 42
    selection environment 24, 42
    selection in 23
script 58–60
second-order intentions 1
selection 16, 22–25, 41
selection environment, and science 42
self 4, 68
self-efficacy 12
self-interest 72, 80, 88, 90, 91, 101, 107
sense 54–57, 62–63, 64, 70
    clouds of 63
    and meaning 4
    and metaphor 57
    and poetry 57, 61–62
sentences and word meaning 56–57
Shaftesbury, Earl of 90
Sherman, Lawrence W. 85
single-channel rival system 23–24
Smith, Adam 102

social media 38, 105–6
society 67
socioeconomics
    evolution, compared with biological evolution 17
    failure of interactors under selection 22–23
    phenomena 16
    and replication 25
    variation 26
solidarity 105
Soviet Union 36
speech acts 53
speech and writing, difference between 57–58
Spender, J. C. 41
stereotypes 93–94
Strang, Heather 85
structural change 45–46, 49, 60
subconsciousness 56, 69
subject 4
subsidiary assumptions 29, 30, 50
Sugden, Robert 99, 102
symbolic capital 77
symbols 83
synthetic truth 51

tacit ideology 106
tacit knowledge 31, 50
Taoism 3
Teece, D. 43, 44
Theil, Henri 34
theory, falsification of 30
thymos 11–12, 67, 98
time 10
totalitarianism 99
transactional relations 100
transmission 16
trust 95, 100–5

truth 4, 51, 72
Tsoukas, Haridimos 6, 38

uncertainty 49–51, 78
unconsciousness 56
universal basic income (UBI) 110–11
universal Darwinism 16–19, 27
universalism 96
universality 5–6
utilitarianism 94
utility ethics 94

variation 25–27
    blindness 47–48
    and collaboration 50–51
variety generation 15, 16, 17
Veblen, T. 87
virtual innateness 92
virtues 89, 91–92, 94, 96–97. *See also* courage; justice; moderation; reason

warranted assertion 4, 51
Weber, Max 81
Welzel, Christian 74–75
Winter, Sidney 21, 26, 44
Witt, Ulrich 23, 27, 39
Wittgenstein, Ludwig 32, 53, 54, 55, 58
word and sentence, relation between 55
World Value Survey (WVS) 74–75
writing and speech, difference between 57–58

Yamagishi, M. 103
Yamagishi, T. 103
Yin and Yang cycle 47

Zollo, M. 44

www.ingramcontent.com/pod-product-compliance
Lightning Source LLC
Chambersburg PA
CBHW021145230426
43667CB00005B/262